BUDDHIST
FAITH *in* AMERICA

MICHAEL BURGAN

J. GORDON MELTON, SERIES EDITOR

Facts On File, Inc.

BUDDHIST FAITH IN AMERICA

Faith in America

Facts On File, Inc.

132 West 31st Street

New York, NY 10001

Library of Congress Cataloging-in-Publication Data

Burgan, Michael.
      Buddhist faith in America. / Michael Burgan.
        p. cm. — (Faith in America)
      Includes bibliographical references and index.
      ISBN 0-8160-4988-2
      1. Buddhism—United States. 2. Asians—United States—Religion.
      I. Title. II. Series.

      BQ732.B87 2003
      294'0973—dc21   2003040815

Facts On File books are available at special discounts when purchased in bulk quantities for businesses, associations, institutions, or sales promotions. Please call our Special Sales Department in New York at (212) 967-8800 or (800) 322-8755.

You can find Facts On File on the World Wide Web at http://www.factsonfile.com

Produced by the Shoreline Publishing Group LLC
Editorial Director: James Buckley Jr.
Contributing Editor: Beth Adelman
Designed by Thomas Carling, Carling Design, Inc.
Photo research by Laurie Schuh
Index by Nanette Cardon, IRIS

Photo credits:
Cover: AP/Wide World (main, bottom left); Don Farber (bottom center, bottom right).
AP/Wide World: 37, 53, 55, 58, 72, 82, 94, 99, 103; Art Resource 46; Bridgeman Art Library 11; Kokaku Blix 76;
Tom Carling 100; Corbis 24; Courtesy Shambhala: 91; Courtesy Tibet House: 94; Digital Stock 6, 14;
Don Farber, 32, 35, 60, 69, 70, 86, 96; Getty Images 49, 79; Giraudon/Art Resource, NY 17;
Library of Congress 29; Marcia Lippman 70; North Wind Archives: 20; Shooting Star/Touchstone Pictures
46; Timepix/Copyright Time Inc. 44; Barbara Weinstein 66.

Printed in the United States of America.

VB 10 9 8 7 6 5 4 3 2 1

This book is printed on acid-free paper.

CONTENTS

FOREWORD

AMERICA BEGINS A NEW MILLENNIUM AS ONE OF THE MOST RELIGIOUSLY diverse nations of all time. Nowhere else in the world do so many people—offered a choice free from government influence—identify with such a wide range of religious and spiritual communities. Nowhere else has the human search for meaning been so varied. In America today, there are communities and centers for worship representing all of the world's religions.

The American landscape is dotted with churches, temples, synagogues, and mosques. Zen Buddhist zendos sit next to Pentecostal tabernacles. Hasidic Jews walk the streets with Hindu swamis. Most amazing of all, relatively little conflict has occurred among religions in America. This fact, combined with a high level of tolerance of one another's beliefs and practices, has let America produce people of goodwill ready to try to resolve any tensions that might emerge.

The Faith in America series celebrates America's diverse religious heritage. People of faith and ideals who longed for a better world have created a unique society where freedom of religious expression is a keynote of culture. The freedom that America offers to people of faith means that not only have ancient religions found a home here, but that newer forms of expressing spirituality have also taken root. From huge churches in large cities to small spiritual communities in towns and villages, faith in America has never been stronger. The paths that different religions have taken through American history is just one of the stories readers will find in this series.

Like anything people create, religion is far from perfect. However, its contribution to the culture and its ability to help people are impressive, and these accomplishments will be found in all the books in the series. Meanwhile, awareness and tolerance of the different paths our neighbors take to the spiritual life has become an increasingly important part of citizenship in America.

Today, more than ever, America as a whole puts its faith in freedom—the freedom to believe.

Buddhist Faith in America

Though only becoming widely visible in America in the last half of the 20th century, Buddhism first appeared in the country in the middle of the 19th century when Chinese immigrants who practiced Buddhism were attracted to California by news of the gold strike of 1849. After a hopeful beginning, however, much of the next century of Buddhist participation in American life included discrimination and persecution. Buddhists of Asian background became the subjects of legislation aimed at excluding them from the American dream. These actions culminated in the wholesale uprooting of Japanese Americans from their homes and resettlement in internment camps during World War II.

In spite of the obstacles, Japanese and Chinese Buddhist Americans found a place to thrive in America and watched through the 20th century as the popular culture transformed their community from an object of derision to one of admiration. Soon after World War II, Americans who had discovered Buddhism as a result of their wartime travels in Asia returned to introduce Buddhism to a new generation of seekers.

Then, in 1965, everything changed. The legislation blocking the entrance of Asians to America was removed and Buddhist practitioners arrived from across Asia, from countries such as Sri Lanka, Myanmar (Burma), Cambodia, Vietnam, Hong Kong, Korea, and Tibet. With Buddhist teachers from all the major traditions suddenly available, Americans from a broad spectrum of backgrounds sought spiritual enlightenment. During the last decades of the 20th century, Buddhism experienced spectacular growth and an unprecedented acceptance in American society and culture. *Buddhist Faith in America* explores this new religious community and the contribution it is already making to American diversity.

— *J. Gordon Melton, Series Editor*

INTRODUCTION

A Prince and His Path

A YOUNG PRINCE FROM INDIA TURNS HIS BACK ON WEALTH AND power to live as a pauper and seek the meaning of life, pain, and death. During his travels, he studies with wise men and endures physical suffering designed to purify his mind. Finally, the former prince decides that neither vast riches nor severe self-tortures can help people answer life's deepest questions. Instead, he calls for a middle way between the two, and he begins to meditate. Reaching a state of perfect inner calm, the prince becomes the "enlightened one"—the Buddha.

This story might seem like a legend, but the young prince was a real person, and millions of people around the world, known as Buddhists, believe he did find a way to reach enlightenment, a state in which people can escape the suffering caused by craving, hatred, and ignorance. Reaching enlightenment also leads to nirvana, or the ending of the cycle of death and rebirth. Buddhists follow the teachings of this young prince, who was known as Siddhartha Gautama (c.563 B.C.E.–483 B.C.E.) before he became the Buddha.

Buddhism provides a framework for how to live: It teaches compassion, eliminating physical and mental desires, and meditating to reach nirvana and to find the Buddhahood inside everyone. Buddhism is one of the world's great religions, although some people—including a few Buddhists—say it is not really a

Different scholars have come
up with different ways to
label the major groupings of
American Buddhists. Asian
Buddhists who came to the
United States are called
ethnic, immigrant, or cradle
Buddhists. Other immigrants
and native-born Americans
raised in another faith who
later chose Buddhism are
called convert or Western
Buddhists. Some writers also
distinguish between recent
Asian immigrants and the
"Americanized" descendants
of the first Chinese and
Japanese Buddhist
immigrants. This book will
use "ethnic" and "convert" to
distinguish the two major
groups. By one estimate,
the United States has just
under 1 million convert
Buddhists.

PRECEDING PAGE
The founder
*Statues of Buddha, such as
this one from China, often
show him seated. Different
cultures depict the features
of Buddha in different ways.*

religion. Buddhism, these people claim, is a philosophy, or a form of psychology, not a religion in the Western sense, centered around the worship of a universal creator, a God. But Buddhism does have rituals and key elements of faith, and, like Western religions, it provides a way to understand and prepare for the ultimate reality all humans face: physical death.

Buddhism Comes to America

As an Eastern, or Asian, religion, Buddhism's roots in the United States are not as deep as the Judeo-Christian traditions brought to North America by the earliest European settlers. The first practicing Buddhists in the continental United States were Chinese immigrants, drawn to California during the Gold Rush of the 1840s. Over time, however, European Americans (and later, African Americans) began to embrace the Buddha's teachings, adopting and adapting various forms of Buddhism that developed in Asia.

At the start of the 21st century, experts could not pin down the number of Buddhists in America. Some said it was at least 2 or 3 million; others believed it could be as high as 6 million. Most scholars agreed, however, that the number was growing, fueled by Asian Buddhist immigrants and their American-born children, and by a growing interest in the religion among Americans of European and African descent.

Pinning down the numbers is difficult because people cannot agree on who is a Buddhist. People who blend Buddhist thought with Christian beliefs or "new age" practices might or might not call themselves Buddhists. Asians immigrants raised in a Buddhist family might say they are Buddhists, even if they never chant or meditate. By its nature, Buddhism is not caught up in labeling or counting. People's intentions and actions say more about their "Buddhist-ness" then what they call themselves or what others call them.

The number of American Buddhists, however, is not as important as the growing influence Buddhism has in all parts of public life—cultural, social, political—and the inner quiet it provides to its followers. American Buddhists are shaping a new kind of Buddhism in the United States, marked by the introduction of American values and a greater dialogue between the different forms of Asian Buddhism. Before examining Buddhism in American today, we will take a look at the historical Buddha, his teachings, and some of the followers who have shaped this powerful religion.

Siddhartha Seeks the Way

By most accounts, Siddhartha Gautama was born some time in the middle of the sixth century B.C.E. (before the common, or Christian, era). His birth year is often given as 563 B.C.E. His father, Suddhodana, a leader (sometimes called king) of the Sakya (or Shakya) clan, ruled the city of Kapilavastu, which was located near the Himalayas in what is now Nepal, near northern India. According to legend, Suddhodana and his wife, Mayadevi, were told their son would be either a great king or a great saint.

As a young prince, Siddhartha enjoyed a life of comfort, protected from the harsh realities of life, such as poverty and disease. He trained as a warrior and also studied the great Indian religious teaching, the Vedas. These teachings were the foundation of the Upanishads, the major religious writings of Hinduism. Siddhartha understood the Indian concepts of reincarnation and karma. All living things died and were reborn over and over. The endless cycle of rebirths was called *samsara*—the wheel of life and death. Depending on their karma, or the total of their actions in one lifetime, living creatures might be reincarnated as a higher or lower life form. Good actions led to good karma, and movement up to a higher life form. Accumulating bad karma had the opposite result. Good and bad karma also affected a person's fortunes within a single lifetime.

Siddhartha's education was preparing him to some day rule, as his father did, but he was sheltered from the harsh realities most people faced. Legends say that a trip the prince took outside his family's palace changed his life.

Traveling along the road, Siddhartha met a wrinkled old man. Later he saw a sick person, and then mourners gathered around a dead body. Siddhartha had never seen these things before, and he asked his chariot driver to explain them. The servant replied that old age, sickness, and death were part of life for all humans. Finally, the prince met a hermit, a holy man who had given up his possessions so he could seek a path that would take him beyond disease, old age, and death.

The sights startled the prince, who realized for the first time that his royal existence did not reflect the reality of the outside world. And, like the hermit, he decided he should search for a way to move beyond these sufferings. At age 29, Siddhartha left his wife and young son, renounced his claim to the throne and his wealth, and began a quest to find the meaning of existence.

THE LANGUAGES OF BUDDHISM

As Buddhism developed in Asia, Buddhists used several languages to record Buddha's teachings and expand on their beliefs. The earliest Buddhists writings were in the Indian language of Pali. Later texts were written in Sanskrit, another Indian language. Many common Buddhist terms have Pali and Sanskrit forms. *Nibbana* is the Pali word for nirvana. Chinese and Japanese words also appear in Buddhist texts written in English. For example, *ch'an* is a Chinese word that describes the higher mental states reached during meditation. Its Japanese equivalent is zen.

The Awakening

For six years Siddhartha wandered without any possessions, studying with yogis, or Hindu holy men. They taught that experiencing great physical pain could help people find wisdom. Siddhartha also practiced yoga, meditated, and fasted, seeking to understand the true nature of karma, reincarnation, and human existence. His severe lifestyle weakened him, and he realized there had to be a middle path between the comfort of his youth and the torture he had inflicted on himself as a wandering mystic. Siddhartha regained his strength by eating healthy, simple foods, then he sat under a tree and began to meditate.

Siddhartha's meditation gave him the solution for ending *samsara*, and the tree he sat under is now called the Bodhi Tree—"tree of awakening." From that moment on, he was the Buddha, the Awakened or Enlightened One. If people followed his teachings, Buddha said anyone could find enlightenment and reach a state of nirvana, a Sanskrit word meaning "putting out a fire." The Indians believed a flame was freed from its fuel when a fire was extinguished. By attaining nirvana, humans were freed from the wheel of life and death.

The Buddha's First Teachings

Now truly awakened, Buddha began to preach his message in northern India. He wanted others to have the opportunity to reach enlightenment and end *samsara*. Buddha first explained his dharma, or truthful doctrine, at a place called Deer Park, at the city of Benares. In this first sermon, he explained the four basic teachings that Buddhists know as the Four Noble Truths—the core of all forms of Buddhism.

The First Noble Truth, Buddha said, is that the essence of individual human existence is filled with *dukkha*, or suffering. "Birth is painful," Buddha preached in his "Sermon on Benares." "Old age is painful, sickness is painful, death is painful . . . contact with unpleasant things is painful, not getting what one wishes is painful."

The Second Noble Truth is that suffering is caused by craving and desire—the desire for material objects, the desire for emotional support, even the desire to reach nirvana. Once people obtain the things or mental states they crave, they fear losing them and cling to them. Ignorance, Buddha said, is at the root of the craving and clasping, as people fail to realize that nothing is permanent, and that the reality they perceive with their senses is not the true reality.

NAMES OF THE BUDDHA

The enlightened Siddhartha Gautama is known by many names. He is sometimes called just Buddha, though other times he is *the* Buddha, It is important to note that anyone can become a Buddha. He is also called Sakyamuni—"wise one of the Sakya clan." Another name for Buddha is Tathagatha—"thus gone." This name reflects Buddha's liberation from *samsara*.

With the Third Noble Truth, Buddha offered hope to counter the gloomy world view of the first two truths. Humans can end their suffering, he said, when they stop craving and let go of their attachments.

In the Fourth Noble Truth, Buddha said the way to end craving is to follow his Eightfold Path, a list of attitudes and practices that focus a person's life on reaching nirvana. Buddha called his teachings the Middle Way, the path between the extremes of wealth and self-punishment he had experienced before his enlightenment.

Other Teachings

Buddha also explained that humans consist of five basic components, called the Aggregates of Existence. The first is form, or the physical body. The other four are mental states: feeling, perception, tendencies, and consciousness. Although a person's body, thoughts and feelings seem real, Buddha said they ultimately have no substance.

Buddha also addressed karma and rebirth. He said every action has consequences that are not always seen at the time. Every cause has an effect. Good actions bring rewards, in this life and in the ones to

Buddha's classroom
This contemporary Indian painting, called Adoration of the Buddha, *shows Buddha in the traditional seated pose under the Bodhi Tree, surrounded by his followers.*

follow. Bad actions doom people to remain locked in *samsara*. Buddha outlined a series of linked actions that shape all human life, sometimes called the Chain of Causation or the Chain of Dependent Origination. Three links of the chain are particularly important: ignorance, craving, and grasping. Eliminating these are the key to ending the wheel of life and rebirth.

Rebirth occurs for all sentient creatures—any living thing that has senses and awareness—and can take place in worlds of existence other than the one on Earth. Many people in India believed in an assortment of gods, devils, and types of heaven and hell. These beliefs, and the gods of other countries where Buddhism later developed, were sometimes incorporated into Buddhism.

Buddha explored another common issue in Indian thinking of the time: the nature of the self, or soul, called *atman*. Buddha believed in *anatman*, or non-self. A person's physical body and mind are not their true nature, he said. The body is not permanent. Nothing is permanent except the non-self—the essence of each person that can attain nirvana. If people remember that everything is impermanent and the idea of "self" they carry in their heads is not real, they can begin to end their attachment to the world.

Spreading the Word

Buddha's closest followers were *bhikkhus*, or monks. These wandering monks owned next to nothing and begged for their food. Buddha also attracted people who did not give up their daily lives to follow him, but who still embraced his teachings. Buddhism appealed to Indians of all backgrounds. Indian society at the time was divided into specific social classes, or castes. People from one caste did not associate with people from another. Buddhism rejected the strict separation of castes, offering enlightenment to anyone who walked the Middle Path.

In general, however, the monastic life was seen as the most direct way to end *samsara*. The laity—people who did not become monks—did their part by supporting the monks and trying to live by Buddha's teachings. These actions helped the laity accumulate merit, which created good karma.

Monks and laity alike were expected to follow the Five Precepts, or orders: do not kill, do not steal, do not engage in harmful sexual activity, do not lie, do not use intoxicants (alcohol and drugs). Monks could not have sex at all, and other rules for proper behavior were added over the years.

Buddha preached his message for 45 years, gaining many followers along the way. The community of followers was called the *sangha*. (Sometimes the word is used narrowly, to describe the monks or nuns living in a monastery. More broadly, it means a community of believers.) Buddhism began with the life and teachings of the Buddha, as individuals chose to model their lives on his life and accept his teachings.

Nothing Buddha preached was written down in his lifetime. Only after he died did the monks begin to write down his sayings. Some are sutras, or scriptures. Others are short sayings collected in a book called the Dhammapada. These sayings and the sutras are still read and discussed today.

The monks also developed the first Buddhist rituals. The most important was saying the Triratana, or Triple Jewel, when converting to Buddhism: "I take refuge in the Buddha. I take refuge in the dharma. I take refuge in the *sangha*." Buddha, dharma, and *sangha* remain at the heart of Buddhism, and some followers recite the Triple Jewel before meditation and meals.

Buddhism developed alongside Hinduism and the other Indian religions. It began to spread beyond the borders of India under the empire of Ashoka (273–232 B.C.E.), a powerful Indian king. After years of conquest and slaughter, Ashoka converted to Buddhism. Afterward, he ruled by Buddhist principles, stressing nonviolence and compassion. He also sent missionaries to teach Buddhism across southeast Asia. The religion took hold in other parts of India and the neighboring countries of Burma (now Myanmar) and Ceylon (now Sri Lanka). Gradually, Buddhism spread even further across Asia.

The Vehicles of Buddhism

As Buddhism grew, leading monks developed different interpretations of Buddha's teachings and the writings about them that were recorded after his death. These contrasting views are often called vehicles, because they transport Buddhists from *samsara* to nirvana. Each vehicle has a presence in the United States today, and is followed by both ethnic Buddhists and converts.

Around 200 B.C.E., Buddhists began to split into two major camps. Some wanted to remain true to the original form of Buddhism,

WOMEN IN BUDDHISM

Indian society during Buddha's lifetime was controlled by men, and women had few rights. At first, Buddha only accepted men as followers, but eventually he accepted *bhikkhunis*, or nuns. According to one legend, he relented after his stepmother and aunt led a large group of women asking for acceptance as followers. Buddhist nuns were considered secondary to monks, although today women are taking a greater role in American Buddhism.

Teachers and students
These Thai Buddhist monks stand in front of a beautifully decorated shrine. Note the circular symbols on the doorway, which reflect the Buddhist idea of the "wheel of life."

stressing the importance of the monastic life. Their Buddhism was called Theravada, or "doctrine of the elders," and they followed the teachings set down in texts written in Pali. Theravada was most influential in Burma, Thailand, Laos, Cambodia, and Sri Lanka. Its teachings on meditation, called *vipassana*, are well-known in the West. Sometimes taught outside of a Buddhist framework, *vipassana* is also known as insight meditation. In Buddhist traditions, most forms of meditation are done while sitting cross-legged on a mat or cushion.

The other Buddhist group focused on the wisdom revealed in several different sutras written in Sanskrit. These Buddhists believed their faith could be understood and appreciated without one becoming a monk. The people in this group called their ideas Mahayana, or "greater vehicle," and they sometimes insulted Theravada Buddhism by labeling it Hinayana, or "lesser vehicle." Mahayana Buddhism primarily flourished in China, Japan, Korea, and Vietnam. Mahayana practitioners tried to bring Buddhism to common people, and they encouraged a blending of Buddhist practices and beliefs with native religions.

A third vehicle is Vajrayana—the "diamond vehicle." It emerged later out of both Theravada and Mahayana teachings, although it is sometimes considered a form of Mahayana. Vajrayana also borrowed elements of Hinduism and blended with the native religions of central Asia north of India. The name reflects the belief that the essence of the universe is clear and unchanging, like a diamond. Vajrayana has a wider range of rituals and symbols than the other two vehicles, and it is most closely associated with Tibet.

The Essence of Mahayana

The Mahayana Buddhists both built on existing Theravadin beliefs and introduced new concepts. Theravada champions the *arhat*—the wise man who focuses on meditation as the way to achieve nirvana for himself in his current lifetime. Mahayana stresses the role of enlightened people who choose to postpone reaching nirvana. They remain in *samsara* so they can help others reach enlightenment. These compassionate beings are called bodhisattvas. Their goal is to achieve Buddhahood (the perfect state all humans have within them) and enlightenment, and then show compassion to others, as Buddha himself did. The most famous bodhisattva is Avalokiteshvara, a possibly mythological figure also called Kuan Yin in Chinese and Kannon in Japanese. Known as the Bodhisattva of Compassion, this holy figure is often represented as a woman.

Mahayana also does not accept the traditional Buddhist view on duality, or the existence of opposites. *Samsara* and nirvana are one pair of opposites. So are *atman* and *anatman*. But the Mahayana philosophy does not distinguish between opposites, instead stressing nonduality. Everything is the same, because everything, even nirvana, is *sunyata*, or emptiness. But this emptiness does not mean the physical

SAYINGS OF BUDDHA
Here is a selection of passages from the Dhammapada:

One is not wise merely because he talks much. But he who is calm, free from hatred and fear, is verily called a wise man.

A disciplined mind brings happiness.

"All forms of existence are unreal"; he who perceives the truth of this gets disgusted with this world of suffering. This is the path to purity.

world is not real, and the emptiness is not, as Buddhist scholar James William Coleman notes in his book, *The New Buddhism* (2001), a "blank nothingness." *Sunyata* is outside the human intellectual concept of real and non-real. Everything that happens or appears has no built-in meaning of its own. Everything humans experience is just a brief representation of "a stream of endless transformation," as American Zen master Philip Kapleau (b.1912) writes in his book *Zen: Merging of East and West* (published in 1989). "Though *sunyata* is without form, it informs everything; to see into this no-thingness of things is awakening." Exploring *sunyata* and other Mahayana concepts is difficult for many Westerners raised to see duality and the concrete nature of the physical world as the only reality.

Mahayana Buddhists also believe a person can use prayers and the help of bodhisattvas and buddhas as they seek enlightenment. Theravada, on the other hand, stresses the individual nature of that quest—believers should strive for nirvana on their own, through meditation. Although the Buddha did not become a god in Mahayana thought, he is sometimes seen as more than a mere human. Theravada, however, never raised Buddha to the level of divine or gave him godlike qualities.

The Forms of Mahayana

As it developed, Mahayana took different forms in different lands. In China, two popular forms were Pure Land and Ch'an Buddhism. Pure Land is centered around the Buddha Amitabha (Buddha of Boundless Life). Its followers believe that by calling on Amitabha, they will enter the Pure Land, a sort of paradise, after they die. The Chinese Buddhists devoted to Amitabha chant the phrase Namo A-mit'o Fo—"Hail Amida Buddha!"

Putting less emphasis on meditation and deep philosophical teachings, Pure Land Buddhism gained strength among the common people of China, and later Japan. The Japanese version was shaped by a monk named Shinran (1173–1263), and is called Shin Buddhism. Various other sects formed out of Shin, including Jodo Shinshu, which Japanese immigrants brought to the United States in the 19th century.

Ch'an Buddhism also developed in China before having a strong impact on Japan. In 520, a great Buddhist teacher named Bodhidharma (c.470–543) traveled from India to China. This Mahayana monk

---

THE BODHISATTVA VOW

Many Mahayana Buddhists chant the Bodhisattva vow, indicating their willingness to help others as they seek enlightenment:

All beings, without number, I vow to liberate.

Endless blind passions I vow to uproot.

Dharma gates, beyond measure, I vow to penetrate.

The Great Way of Buddha I vow to attain.

Japanese Buddha
This painting is called
The Paradise of Amida.
Amida is the center of the
Pure Land school of
Japanese Buddhism,
and represents beauty
and wisdom.

stressed deep meditation as the path to nirvana. In China, his form of Buddhism is called Ch'an, and in Japan it is called Zen. Most American Buddhists in this tradition follow one of the two major Japanese schools of Zen—Rinzai and Soto—although Ch'an and Korean Zen centers also exist. Japanese Zen also includes Sanbo Kyodan, or Three Treasures Association, which blends elements of Soto and Rinzai. This lay organization was founded in 1954.

The different forms of Zen—and of other Mahayana practices—are sometimes called lineages. Teachers in a lineage pass dharma transmission to selected students, meaning the students have mastered the lineage's practices and can become teachers themselves.

Zen, unlike Pure Land, appealed to Japanese intellectuals and the warrior class—the samurai. It grapples with difficult philosophical questions about the nature of reality and understanding. In Rinzai Buddhism, masters give students nonsensical or puzzling sayings, called koans, to stimulate their understanding of Buddhahood and prod their awakening. The Soto school places more emphasis on long sessions of meditation, called *zazen*. Meditators empty their minds of all thoughts and images. They can continue their practice while walking, and Zen masters encourage Buddhists to empty their mind while doing daily activities, so that whatever they do has their complete attention.

In Japan, Zen and Shin developed along with another branch of Mahayana Buddhism, called Nichiren. This tradition is named for its founder, Nichiren (1222–1282). A former monk, he did not see the worth of other forms of Buddhism and actively sought to convert others to his teachings. Nichiren also used chanting as a key method for reaching enlightenment. He urged followers to chant from the Lotus Sutra, one of the most famous writings in Mahayana Buddhism. Nichiren takes several forms today.

In the United States, Soka Gakkai International (SGI) is the largest Nichiren branch. Its goals, according to the SGI-USA web site (www.sgi-usa.org), are "world peace and individual happiness." The other major branch is the Nichiren Soshu Temple. Soka Gakkai was once part of the Nichiren Soshu Temple, acting as the lay recruiting arm and emphasizing social reform. The Nichiren Soshu temple, led by priests, focuses on leading temple rituals. The two groups split in 1991, and they still have a tense relationship.

The Special Case of Tibet

As we've already mentioned, Vajrayana Buddhism is closer to Mahayana than Theravada, but it is distinct enough to deserve its own section. Today, for most Westerners, Vajrayana really means Tibetan Buddhism, since it is the best-known form of this third vehicle. Japan, however, also has a form of Vajrayana called Shingon.

Tibetan Buddhists combined practices from Hindu yogis with their native Bon religion. The result was a Buddhism more colorful and supernatural than the other two vehicles. Tibetan Buddhism is sometimes called Tantric Buddhism. Tantra is a sacred text or teaching, although not all tantras are Buddhist. Tantric Buddhists believe

HONORING THE BUDDHA

After his death, Buddha was cremated and his followers placed his relics, or bodily remains, under sacred mounds, called stupas. These shrines, which are also made for other holy people, exist across Asia, and there are about 50 in the United States.

they sometimes have to go beyond the traditional Buddhist teachings to find enlightenment. This can mean breaking the precepts that forbid alcohol or sex. This approach is also sometimes called "crazy wisdom." One ancient Tantric text says, "The wise man renders himself free of impurity by means of impurity itself."

In meditation, the Tibetans use visualization, or imaging certain colors or images. Some of the symbols used in visualization and in Tibetan art are called mandalas. These detailed images represent gods and forces in the universe. The Tibetan Buddhists also chant mantras, which are specific sounds designed to help achieve awakening. Special body positions, called *mutras*, have the same effect. Following Tantric practices, its followers believe, can lead to enlightenment in one lifetime, rather than enduring *samsara* for many reincarnations.

Tibetan Buddhism is centered around teachers, called gurus or, more commonly, lamas. They became political as well as spiritual leaders. Many lamas are considered to be *tulkus*, or reincarnated lamas. Young children who are identified as *tulkus* are taken from their families to receive special religious training. Some teachings remain secret, as lamas learn seemingly magical ways to enter trances or raise their body temperatures.

Tibetan Buddhism eventually split into four distinct orders of monks: Gelugpa, Sakyapa, Nyingma, and Kagyupa. (There is also a movement based outside these four traditions, which combines their teachings, called Rimé.) Nyingma and Kagyupa focus more on meditation and tantric practices. Gelugpa and Sakyapa are more oriented toward scholarly study. The Dalai Lama, also known as Tenzin Gyatso (b.1935), perhaps the most famous Buddhist leader in the world, belongs to the Gelugpa order.

The Dalai Lama's popularity and the political issue of China's dominance over Tibet gives Tibetan Buddhism a large share of media attention in the West. But the Vajrayana vehicle is just one small part of the rich religious heritage begun by the historical Buddha more than 2,500 years ago.

THE MYSTERIOUS KOANS

Koans, called *kung-ans* in Chinese, can be as simple as, "What is *mu* (mind)?" Others are small stories that present a problem the student must consider. Once students believe they understand a koan, they meet with their teachers to discuss it. Koans can be answered in many ways.

Buddhism Comes to America

THE TWO CULTURAL STRAINS OF AMERICAN BUDDHISM—ETHNIC and convert—began to develop in the United States at about the same time. In 1849, the first Chinese immigrants reached California looking for work and wealth during the Gold Rush. By then, several native-born American writers and thinkers were exploring Asian religious teachings, including Buddhism. These writers did not actually convert to Buddhism, but they made the first attempts to reflect Buddhist ideas in American intellectual life, and they influenced future generations of writers.

For both convert and ethnic Buddhists, the turn of the 19th century saw a growing Buddhist presence in the United States—but one still beyond the recognition of most Americans. Asian Buddhist communities were centered in certain neighborhoods in large cities—"Chinatowns" or "Japantowns" that were not the tourist attractions they often are today. There, the immigrants and their descendants set up the first Buddhist temples. Outside of these communities, Buddhism was largely known only to scholars and the handful of American religious seekers who embraced the dharma (see page 23).

Among converts, Buddhism's larger cultural importance came after World War II. A new intellectual and artistic movement, the Beat Generation, stirred interest in Buddhism and influenced the "counterculture" that

PRECEDING PAGE
Working on the railroad
This woodcut from the 1880s shows Chinese workers wearing traditional hats in the process of breaking rocks and tunneling, while helping to build the Transcontinental Railroad.

developed in the 1960s. Seeking to counter the dominant American values of materialism and competition, many young Americans found wisdom in a religion that tried to eliminate craving and promote compassion.

The 1960s also marked a turning point for ethnic Buddhism in the United States, as new immigration laws increased the number of people arriving from Asia. The aftermath of the Vietnam War also played a part, as refugees came seeking freedom and economic opportunity. Immigrants from Asia continue to arrive in the United States in large numbers, leading to questions about the compatibility of the different schools of Buddhist teaching and the relations between the two cultural strains that flourish today in the United States.

First Arrivals

The first Asian Buddhists in the United States were Chinese immigrants. Just five years after the first Chinese reached California, the state had more than 13,000 Chinese residents, and by 1870 the total number in the United States, mostly in the West, was more than 66,000. (Many of these later immigrants came to build railroads.)

The first Buddhist temples appeared in San Francisco in the early 1850s, built by Chinese merchant organizations formed to address the social and economic needs of their community. The Buddhism practiced in these temples often combined elements of other Chinese religions. Practitioners also freely mixed different strains of Mahayana teaching. As Chinese Buddhists spread throughout the West, they set up small temples in homes or built small shacks for their religious services.

The Chinese immigrants faced extreme prejudice, because many Americans believed they took jobs from European- and native-born workers. Nativists—the outspoken opponents of immigration—also thought Chinese culture, including its religions, was too foreign and conflicted with American values. In 1882, Congress passed the Chinese Exclusion Act, forbidding new Chinese immigration. The Chinese population began to fall, and Chinese Buddhism in the United States lost influence. By the 1930s, many former Buddhist temples had been sold or abandoned. Chinese Mahayana Buddhism did not revive until the 1960s.

The Japanese Experience

The first organized migrations to Hawaii and the mainland came after 1868, and more came after 1885, when Japan allowed open emigration to

America for the first time. The first official Japanese Buddhist presence was in Hawaii in 1889 (nine years before the islands became a U.S. territory), when the Jodo Shinshu priest Soryu Kagahi arrived. He set up a temple before returning to Japan. Another priest arrived in 1897, and two years later, the first two Jodo Shinshu priests arrived on the U.S. mainland, in San Francisco. Japanese residents in the area had already set up the Young Men's Buddhist Association, similar to the Young Men's Christian Associations (YMCA) common in many U.S. cities. Later, a Young Women's Buddhist Association was also formed.

The two Jodo Shinshu priests were Dr. Shuye Sonoda and Reverend Kakuryo Nishijima. They were the first Buddhist religious officials to become permanent U.S. residents. The two priests helped set up what became the Buddhist Mission of North America (BMNA). Although called a mission, BMNA was primarily geared toward serving the religious needs of Japanese immigrants, not to converting Americans. The mission set up programs to help the Japanese and their children assimilate to American culture. Sonoda also helped start the first Buddhist organization in the United States for converted Buddhists, the Dharma Sangha of Buddha.

As with the Chinese, Japanese immigrants eventually faced legal limits. The so-called "Gentlemen's Agreement" of 1907 between the United States and Japan ended the emigration of unskilled Japanese workers to America. The agreement, however, did allow family members of Japanese-Americans to come to the United States. Thousands of women in Japan married men living in America, and then joined their husbands. Unlike the Chinese, the Japanese population was not dominated by elderly single men; instead, families developed, and their Buddhist institutions remained fairly strong. All Japanese immigration stopped in 1924 with the passage of an American law that virtually ended emigration from Asia. Japanese Buddhist temples and societies developed without a continuing infusion of new arrivals from Japan.

The Early Convert Experience

By the mid 1800s, translations of Buddhist and Hindu texts were becoming more common in the West, available to scholars and writers. To some Christian eyes, Buddhism seemed negative, with its emphasis on suffering and nothingness. Early students of Buddhism often did not go beyond these ideas to see the more positive side of this foreign faith.

BUDDHIST EXPLORERS IN NORTH AMERICA?

According to a few scholars, the first Buddhists may have reached North America hundreds of years before Christopher Columbus arrived in 1492. The theory was first discussed in Europe during the 18th century, when French scholar Joseph de Guignes (1759–1845) found a Chinese document recounting the voyage of a Buddhist monk to a land called Fu-sang. The description of the country convinced de Guignes that Fu-sang was Mexico, and other scholars noted a similarity between Chinese Buddhist art and architecture and the temples built by some of Mexico's native people. In recent years, some Chinese scholars have continued to study the possibility of ancient links between China and the Americas.

History comes alive
This Buddhist temple in the Valley of the Temples on the island of Oahu in Hawaii is a replica of the 12th-century Byodo-In Temple in Uji, Japan. Japanese Buddhism has a very strong presence in Hawaii.

Some Americans, however, did see the value of Buddhism and related to the Buddha's teaching on the oneness of human experience. Ralph Waldo Emerson (1803–1882), a minister, writer, and philosopher from Massachusetts, was one important thinker who explored Buddhism and other Eastern religions. Emerson was at the heart of a literary and philosophical movement called Transcendentalism, which stressed a mystical connection with nature and the universe. Henry David Thoreau (1817–1862) was another Transcendentalist who turned to Buddhism, and Emerson's ideas influenced the poet Walt Whitman (1819–1892).

Emerson had mixed feelings about Buddhism, as noted by Buddhist historian Rick Fields in his book *How the Swans Came to the Lake* (1992). Field quotes Emerson's journals in which Emerson called Buddhism "remorseless" and that the idea of annihilation (nirvana) left him cold. Another time, however, he wrote, "the Buddhist is a Transcendentalist." Emerson also expressed ideas that could be called Buddhist. In his essay "The Over-Soul," he talks about "the universal sense of want and ignorance"—similar to the craving and ignorance the Buddha warned against. Emerson also says that "within man is the soul of the whole…the eternal ONE." This goes along with many Mahayana teachings that stress the connection of everything in the universe. The seeming distinction between an individual and what he or she sees as the "outside world" is an illusion—an illusion that is shattered as a person reaches enlightenment.

Emerson and others who explored Buddhism were not converts. But during the 1870s, some European Americans did embrace the dharma more fully. One of the best-known was Henry Steel Olcott (1832–1907). He, along with a Russian immigrant named Helena Petrovna Blavatsky (1831–1891), founded the Theosophical Society in 1875. Blavatsky was an occultist—someone who believed it was possible to communicate with the spirits of dead people. The Theosophical Society blended Eastern religious teachings, particularly Buddhism, with occultist beliefs.

Olcott traced his roots to the Puritans who settled New England in the 17th century. Raised a Presbyterian, he gave up Christianity as a young man. When he turned to Buddhism, Olcott said he wanted to promote a "pure" form of the religion, one that was true to the Buddha's teachings. In 1880, Olcott and Blavatsky went to Ceylon (now called Sri Lanka) and took the Buddhist vows of the Three Refuges (the Triple Jewel, see page 13) and the Five Precepts (see page 12). They were the first European-Americans to publicly declare their faith in Buddhism. Olcott helped spark a revival of Buddhism in Ceylon, earning him the nickname "the White Buddhist."

Back in the United States, the Theosophical Society helped spread Buddhist ideas to Americans seeking new religious insights.

Meeting of the Religious Minds

The growth of converts to Buddhism in America received a boost from the 1893 World's Parliament of Religions. Held in Chicago, the event coincided with the World's Columbian Exposition, which honored the

400th anniversary of Christopher Columbus's first voyage to North America. Just as Columbus helped link distant continents, the World's Parliament of Religions forged new spiritual connections between Asia and the West.

At the Parliament, representatives from Theravada, Zen, Nichiren, and other Buddhist traditions spoke about their faith. For many Americans, steeped in Judeo-Christian teachings, this was their first exposure to Asian Buddhists and the finer points of the Buddha's teachings.

After the Parliament, some of the Buddhist leaders or their followers remained in the United States and began spreading the dharma. The Parliament also led to the first systematic publication of Buddhist writings in the United States.

Paul Carus (1852–1919), a German immigrant, was a scholar and editor who abandoned Protestantism to seek a religion that could combine the modern ideas of science with spirituality. He attended the Parliament and felt that Buddhism offered the kind of religion he wanted. In his book *Buddhism and Its Christian Critics* (1897), Carus called the Buddha "the first prophet of the religion of science." He began publishing magazines and books that tried to make Buddhism understandable to American readers.

Developments in the Ethnic Communities

Carus's religion of science, and Buddhism in general, appealed mostly to European Americans with an intellectual background. The number of converts was small, and for the first half of the 20th century, ethnic Buddhists remained the major followers of the faith in the United States. The various Chinese and Japanese sects followed the pattern set up at the end of the 19th century: Chinese Buddhism tended to be inclusive, blending different Buddhist strains and elements of other Chinese religions. The Japanese Buddhists usually stayed within the firm boundaries of their particular sect.

Japanese Pure Land Buddhists seemed to reach their peak in the United States around 1930. The sect had 123 ministers; the number fell by more than one-third during the next 50 years. Attendance at dharma schools also peaked around this time. After World War II, many Japanese-Americans spread beyond their base on the West Coast and began pursuing professional careers, weakening ties to their old cultural and religious communities.

BORROWING FOR BUDDHISM

Henry Steel Olcott borrowed from Christian churches the idea of writing a catechism—a series of basic questions with answers that explain a faith. In 1881, Olcott's book *The Buddhist Catechism* first appeared in Sinhalese, the native language of Ceylon, and English. Later the catechism was translated into several Asian languages.

World War II marked an important turning point for Jodo Shin-shu, as the Buddhist Mission for North America was renamed the Buddhist Churches of America (BCA). The change came as Japanese Americans were placed in special camps, called internment camps. The U.S. government feared some Japanese Americans might work with Japan, one of America's enemies in the war, against U.S. interests. Most of the Japanese were U.S. citizens, and they lost their legal rights and their property before entering the camps.

Even before the name change, the BCA tried to become more Americanized by adopting some of the practices used by mainstream Christian religions. Services were held on Sundays, and pews were added to temples. American words, such as *bishop* and *reverend*, replaced traditional Japanese terms.

Postwar Growth Among Converts

After World War II, both convert and ethnic Buddhism began growing slowly in the United States. For many converts, Zen Buddhism was particularly appealing. Several Zen priests had already founded centers to teach meditation. One was located in New York City; another was in California, moving between San Francisco and Los Angeles. Students also discovered Buddhism in books and through lectures.

Zen beliefs shaped the ideas of writers who did not like the direction the United States was taking after World War II. The victory left the United States the strongest country in the world, in terms of its wealth and military power. To some convert Buddhists, Americans seemed too concerned with making money and exercising their power.

A group of writers, sometime called the Beats, spoke out against the excesses they saw around them. Zen Buddhism gave them a different way of looking at the world—one that was foreign to traditional American values. The Beats deliberately tried to set themselves apart from those American values, and Zen gave them tools for doing so. The influence of the Beats helped Zen reach a wider audience. Their work shaped the hippie movement of the 1960s, which opposed America's role in the Vietnam War and suggested meditation (and sometimes drugs) could bring a clearer understanding of reality.

Many converts only dabbled in Buddhism; they did not join monasteries or take lay vows. Others, however, traveled to Asia, steeping themselves in the teachings of Zen and other traditions, especially

ZEN BRIDE AND PRIEST

In 1929, Zen master Sokei-An (1882–1945) opened the Buddhist Society of America in New York City. Sokei-An lectured on Buddhism for the next 12 years. One of the people he influenced was Ruth Fuller (1883–1967). In 1941, she let Sokei-An use her Manhattan home as the society's new headquarters. Fuller and Sokei-An eventually married, and Fuller became a priest at a Japanese Zen temple. She translated several Buddhist texts into English and is considered one of the first important women in American Buddhism. Fuller was also the mother-in-law of Alan Watts (1915–1973), a British writer who published several popular books on Buddhism during the 1950s and 1960s.

Theravada. These more committed converts sparked the growth of convert Buddhism in America during the 1970s and after.

An important new development in convert Buddhism was the arrival of Soka Gakkai. Some Japanese immigrants had brought this form of Nichiren Buddhism with them to the United States, but in 1960, the first American organization was formed. That year, Soka Gakkai president Daisaku Ikeda (b.1928) came to the United States. On his arrival in San Francisco he said, "We have now made the first footprint on this continent, as did Christopher Columbus . . . 20 or 50 years from now, this day will be marked as one of great importance" (his quote comes from *The Faces of Buddhism in America*, 1998, edited by Charles S. Prebish and Kenneth K. Tanaka).

Unlike other Buddhists sects, Soka Gakkai made a strong effort to convert Americans, reaching beyond the Asian immigrant community. Ikeda's group was particularly successful in recruiting urban minorities. Free of some of the strict rules other sects followed, Soka Gakkai was also open to alternative lifestyles, giving it some appeal among gays and lesbians. Soka Gakkai stressed personal development and working toward world peace. By some estimates, Soka Gakkai has attracted more American converts than any other Buddhist sect.

Changes in the Mahayana Ethnic Community

The postwar era also brought changes to the ethnic Buddhist communities. Chinese and Japanese immigration rose after the war (more so for the Japanese), and a new burst of Asian Buddhist immigration began during the 1960s. Old Buddhist sects started to revive, and new organizations formed.

Prominent Chinese Buddhist groups included the Sino-American Buddhist Association, the Buddhist Association of the United States (BAUS), the International Buddhist Progress Society (also called Fo Kuang Shan), and the Institute of Buddhist Culture. Most of the groups focused on the ethnic community, but converts were generally welcome. BAUS, based in New York, built a temple with a 37-foot-tall statue of a sitting Buddha—the largest in the Western Hemisphere. Fo Kuang Shan built a $30-million temple in California and started branch temples in several other major cities. It has led efforts to bring together American Buddhists of all schools.

Temple in the camp
At relocation camps during World War II, such as Manzanar in southern California, Japanese Americans tried to recreate some semblance of normal life, which included setting up Buddhist temples.

Koreans and Vietnamese were among the new Asian immigrants reaching the United States. Many were Christian, but a number were Buddhist, especially among the Vietnamese. The first Korean Buddhist temple opened in Los Angeles in 1973. Korean Buddhism was strongly influenced by Chinese Buddhism. It developed both a meditative approach, taken from Ch'an, and a more devotional style with roots in Pure Land Buddhism. The West Coast temples featured chanting, reading sacred texts, and a sermon.

In other parts of the United States, the Ch'an tradition—called S'on in Korean—developed under the guidance of several masters. From his base in Toronto, Samu Sunim (b.1941) created the Buddhist Society for Compassionate Wisdom. Even better known is the Kwan Um School of Zen, with headquarters in Rhode Island. Kwan Um was founded by Seung Sahn Sunim (b.1927) in 1983, after he had been teaching in the United States for more than a decade. Like other Zen practices, Kwan Um has appealed to converts more than to ethnic Koreans. But unlike other schools of Zen, Kwan Um has actively sought converts. And Seung Sahn has tried to create a distinct style of American Zen, loosening some of the strict rules found in Korean monasteries.

Vietnamese Buddhism has been primarily geared toward the ethnic Vietnamese community. The first temples were often set up in people's homes or in small stores, just as the Chinese did more than 100 years before. Historically, Vietnam has been influenced by China, and Vietnamese Buddhism shows the same blending of different styles as Chinese Buddhism does. Lay people go to temples weekly, for special services, and to pray. Vietnamese Buddhism does not put much stress on meditation, although there is a small Zen tradition. Temples and rituals help Vietnamese immigrants keep cultural ties to their homeland.

Just as the Chinese and Japanese dealt with racial prejudice in the 19th century, more recent Asian immigrants have faced suspicion and hatred. In some cases, native-born Americans fear losing jobs to immigrants. Some Americans distrust the different culture and religious beliefs the Asians bring. Vietnamese Buddhist immigrants have been criticized for their "foreign" beliefs.

In his book *The Vietnamese Experience in America* (1992), Paul James Rutledge writes about some of the interactions between these immigrants and native-born Americans. During the 1980s, a growing Vietnamese community in Oklahoma City, Oklahoma, led one resident to complain about the "funny religion" and the "funny stuff" the immigrants practiced at their temple. The Vietnamese responded by trying to become more Americanized: at a barbecue, monks wore blue jeans and cooked hot dogs for their American guests.

Because of racial and religious differences, Vietnamese and other ethnic Buddhists have sometimes struggled to feel accepted in their new homeland. But as one Vietnamese Buddhist said, becoming an American gave her and others a unique opportunity. "I love America and I love my religion," she said in Rutledge's book. "To be an American is to be free and to be a Vietnamese is to be a Buddhist. That is why I am both."

Tibetan Buddhism Comes to America

Few, if any, Tibetan Buddhists reached the United States before the 1950s. The first important teacher of Tibetan Buddhism in the United States was actually a Mongolian. Geshe Wangyal (1902–1983) moved to New Jersey in 1955 and later opened a Tibetan monastery there. Wangyal was from the Gelugpa order, but eventually all four Tibetan orders (see page 19) had representatives in the United States. The monks who came tried to help other Tibetans settle in the United States, as well as spread the traditions of Vajrayana Buddhism.

Another Late Arrival

For decades, Mahayana schools dominated American Buddhism. The more traditional Theravada had been represented at the 1893 World's Parliament of Religions, but an ethnic Theravadin community of any size did not emerge until the 1960s. The first temple opened in

Washington, D.C., in 1966. Since then, immigrants from Thailand, Sri Lanka, and other Southeast Asian countries with a Theravada tradition have come to America, primarily to larger, highly populated states (California, New York, Texas.)

Theravada Buddhism revolves around the monastic life, and some monks have had trouble adapting to a faster-paced American culture. Finding enough monks for Theravada temples has also been a problem, because the children of Asian immigrants have not been drawn to that demanding life. Most monks are recruited from Asia, although a few non-Asian monks have taken the vows. Within their communities, monks sometimes debate how—or if—they should change Theravadin traditions to attract more monks and adapt to American life.

Theravadins have also addressed the role of nuns. An organized structure for *bhikkhunis* died out in Southeast Asia centuries ago, so women have had no official role in Theravada Buddhism. The push for gender equality in all parts of American live has led to the ordination of nuns, begun by Havanpola Ratanasara (1920–2000), a Sri Lankan monk who settled in the United States.

Vipassana, the distinct meditative practice of Theravada, has been influential among convert Buddhists. In the late 1960s and early 1970s, several Americans traveled to Asia and learned the practice, which is usually called insight meditation in the United States. The founders of the insight meditation movement include Jack Kornfield (b.1945) and Ruth Denison (b.1922). In 1995, Kornfield told Buddhist scholar Gil Fronsdal (as reported in the book *The Faces of Buddhism in America*) that he and other early *vipassana* teachers wanted to offer "the powerful practices of insight meditation . . . without the complication of ritual, robes, chanting, and the whole religious tradition." Many people who use insight meditation do not consider themselves Buddhists, and some may not even realize its Buddhist roots.

The emergence of Theravada monasteries brought the oldest form of Buddhism to the United States. Meanwhile, *vipassana* established a secular form of Buddhism. American Buddhists, ethnic and convert, can choose from a wide spectrum for the Buddhism that suits their beliefs. The United States has brought together all the forms of Buddhism in one country for the first time, leading to dialogues among the schools. That interaction promises to create a new form of American Buddhism, and to influence the larger culture as well.

TIBETAN PIONEER

Thirty years before Geshe Wangyal reached the United States, an American scholar helped introduce Westerners to Tibetan Buddhism. Driven by an interest in theosophy, Walter Evans-Wentz (1878–1965) traveled to India around 1920. He met a lama who introduced him to Tibetan Buddhism, and the two men worked on translating several Tibetan texts into English. One of these was the classic Tibetan Book of the Dead, which helps Buddhists prepare for their death and rebirth. Evans-Wentz gave Westerners an understanding of Tibetan Buddhism and made clear its relation to more classical forms of the religion. He wrote in his book *Tibetan Yoga and Secret Doctrine* (1935), "It is only when the West understands the East and the East the West that a culture worthy of the name civilization will be evolved."

2

Key Events in American Buddhism

COMPARED TO THE JUDEO-CHRISTIAN FAITHS, BUDDHISM HAS A short history in the United States. And the relatively small number of Buddhists in the country has kept it beyond the awareness of most Americans. Still, both specific events and more general trends—rooted in larger cultural changes—have influenced the interest in and growth of Buddhism in America. Here is a look at some of the crucial events in American Buddhist history.

The World's Parliament of Religions

In 1890, the United States had a population of slightly less than 63 million. Out of that number, just 107,000 people were Chinese or Japanese—the Americans most likely to embrace Buddhism at that time. Most of these Asian Americans lived in the West, so the country's familiarity with Asian cultures, including Buddhism, was limited. For many European Americans, the 1893 World's Parliament of Religions gave them their first opportunity to see and meet Buddhists and to appreciate the many different traditions that sprang from the Buddha's teachings.

For the Buddhists who attended, the Parliament gave them a chance to educate and perhaps convert Americans. In 1892, a Japanese newspaper wrote that Buddhists could use the conference to "wed the Great Vehicle [Mahayana

Buddhism] to Western thought." The article (quoted in *The Faces of Buddhism in America*) noted that Buddhism could appeal to Americans "conscious of the destruction of the basis of their faith by the forces at work in civilization." Those forces included the rapid industrialization of the country and the rise of scientific thinking.

At the Parliament, several Buddhist speakers tried to demonstrate that their faith did not conflict with modern science or basic American values. Anagarika Dharmapala (1864–1933), a Buddhist from Ceylon, told the audience, "Buddha inculcated the necessity of self-reliance and independent thought"—two traits Americans have often believed defines their national character. Dharmapala also said (as quoted in *The Faces of Buddhism in America*) that Buddhism "accepted the doctrine of evolution as the only true one, with its corollary, the law of cause and effect." Evolution was gaining acceptance in the intellectual community at that time, but it was in conflict with Christian views that took the Biblical account of creation as literal and absolute truth. Dharmapala said Buddhism offered a faith that accepted the truth of the new scientific doctrine.

In a way, Dharmapala and another Buddhist speaker, Soyen Shaku (1858–1919), were turning the tables on the West. For hundreds of years, Protestant and Roman Catholic missionaries had traveled to Asia seeking converts. Now, Dharmapala and Shaku were the missionaries, shaping their definitions of Buddhist thought to appeal to a foreign audience.

Shaku was a Rinzai Zen monk from Japan and was the first Zen priest to come to America. He used logical arguments to explain Buddhist ideas on the nature of the universe and the law of cause and effect. Causality, he said (as quoted in *The Faces of Buddhism in America*), is "the law of nature, independent of the will of Buddha, and still more of the will of human beings." The universe, once begun, progresses on its own, outside the influence of a divine creator.

Unlike Dharmapala, Shaku could not speak English and relied on translators when he spoke. The language barrier may have reduced his effectiveness, but in the years after the Parliament, Shaku and several of his students had a deep impact among convert Buddhists.

The Foundation of American Zen

Shaku returned to the United States in 1905 to visit friends in California and lecture across the country. Traveling with him was his disciple

Light up the night
Japanese-American children participate here in the Senshin Buddhism candle ceremony that honors the dead.

Nyogen Senzaki (1876–1958). Another disciple, D. T. Suzuki (1870–1966), had already come to the United States to work with publisher Paul Carus on translating Buddhist texts into English. Senzaki and Suzuki helped introduce two sides of Zen Buddhism to America: one devoted to meditation, and the other more intellectual and philosophical.

One of Suzuki's jobs was translating his master's American lectures, which were published as *Sermons of a Buddhist Abbot* (and later released in 1974 as *Zen for Americans*). Suzuki wrote in *Zen for Americans* that he took Shaku's "too Buddhistic" expressions, ideas that would only make sense to a life-long student of the dharma, and made them "more conventional and comprehensible . . . for the benefit of the American public." Suzuki continued that effort throughout his life, and his writings gave many Westerners their first understanding of Zen. Scholar James William Coleman, in his book *The New Buddhism*, writes that Suzuki "probably did more than any other single individual to introduce Zen Buddhism to the West."

Senzaki once studied with Suzuki, but their paths diverged in the United States. While Suzuki became a well-known scholar, Senzaki spent many years working odd jobs and practicing zazen (see page 18). For some unknown reason, Shaku had told his student to wait 20 years before beginning to teach in America. Senzaki followed this request, then began teaching *zazen* in California. Japanese Buddhists gather to meditate in a hall called a zendo. Senzaki called his school the "floating zendo," because he moved his teaching among various buildings in San Francisco and Los Angeles.

Senzaki taught a number of Americans about Zen, and he also brought over several other teachers. Like the speakers at the 1893 Parliament, Senzaki saw a natural link between Zen and the attitudes common in the United States. "The brighter one polishes his mind-mirror of reason," he wrote (as quoted in the Spring 1993 issue of *Tricycle*), "the more the value of Zen can be appreciated. Because Zen is fact and not 'religion' in the conventional sense of the term, the American mind, with its scientific cast, takes to it readily."

The Zen "Boom" of the 1950s and 1960s

While ethnic Buddhists in America continued to follow the different forms of Buddhism practiced for hundreds or thousands of years, Zen became the school of choice for more native-born Americans. Part of this sprang from the work of D. T. Suzuki and his writings and teachings. Part of it was based on the rise of the Beat Generation (see page 27), the post-World War II writers and artists who embraced Buddhist teachings, particularly Zen, in their quest to find deeper meaning in life. The best-known Beat Buddhists were Jack Kerouac (1922–1969), Gary Snyder (b.1930), and Allen Ginsberg (1926–1997). Kerouac, like other young Americans, was introduced to Buddhism through *A Buddhist Bible*. This collection of Theravada and Mahayana teachings was published in 1934 by Dwight Goddard, a Baptist missionary who converted to Buddhism.

The Beat writers sometimes blended different forms of Buddhism, but their brand of the religion was sometimes called "Beat Zen." Kerouac titled one of his books *The Dharma Bums* and wrote a biography of Gautama Siddhartha. Snyder, a poet, eventually went to live in a Japanese Zen monastery and used Buddhist ideas in his work. Ginsberg, another poet, remained a Buddhist throughout his life, and became especially interested in Tibetan Buddhism as taught by Chogyam Trungpa (1939–1987). The Beat writers helped spark an interest in Buddhism among some baby boomers, the Americans born between 1946 and 1964.

Another important source on Buddhism for Americans was Alan Watts. An Englishman who lived in both New York and California, Watts dismissed Beat Zen. He thought most Beats did not dig deeply enough into the meaning of Zen. But Watts also thought traditional Japanese Zen—what he called "square Zen"—was not the answer for Americans seeking enlightenment.

In his writings and his life, Watts did not always emphasize meditation, and he borrowed from other Eastern religions in addition to Buddhism. In one of his early articles, written in 1941 (and quoted in Rick Fields's 1992 book, *How the Swans Came to the Lake*), Watts wrote, "Zen, Jodo Shinshu, and Christianity were all approaching the same point by different routes." Although not a "pure" Zen Buddhist, Watts's many books introduced millions of Westerners to Buddhism.

ADAPTING ZEN

Nyogen Senzaki thought sitting cross-legged on the floor for zazen would be too foreign—or difficult—for his American students, so he let them meditate while sitting on folding chairs.

Keeping the Beat
Author Jack Kerouac was heavily influenced by Zen Buddhism in his writings, such as the novels On the Road *and* Dharma Bums*.*

In 1958, *Time* magazine featured Watts after the publication of his best-known book, *The Way of Zen*. The magazine seemed to dismiss the new interest in Buddhism, calling it "chic." Convert Buddhists have sometimes had to wrestle with the perception that their interest in Buddhism is a mere fad, not a committed devotion to the faith. Mainstream media sometimes seem to have trouble accepting the idea that European Americans or other non-Asians in the West would truly embrace a "foreign" religion.

American Zen Centers Take Root

World War II itself had an impact on Buddhism in America—one that did not fully develop until the 1950s and 1960s. The war brought many native-born Americans to Asia. Some of them explored Buddhism for the first time and studied in Asia after the war. Two important early convert Zen Buddhists, Philip Kapleau (b. 1912) and Robert Aitken (b.1917), had this experience.

At the end of World War II, Kapleau worked as a court reporter at war crimes trials held in Tokyo, Japan. Wanting to better understand Japanese culture, he began studying Zen Buddhism. Kapleau eventually spent 13 years in Japan, studying both Rinzai and Soto Zen. Back in the United States, he started the Rochester Zen Center in 1966, the year after he published *The Three Pillars of Zen*. At the time, Kapleau's book was the most complete look at Zen written by a European American. It eventually sold more than 150,000 copies and was translated into several European languages.

Kapleau also lectured around the country and wrote several other books that expressed his desire to make Zen more suitable for Americans. Kapleau believed that "so long as Zen bore the clear stamp of its Japanese cultural roots, critics in the West would inevitably denigrate it as a 'foreign religion.'" His efforts were meant to "blunt such a criticism" by "experiment[ing] widely with new expressions more congenial to our Western cultural tradition" (this essay was quoted in *Zen: Merging of East and West*, 1989).

Kapleau's teachers included Hakuun Yasutani (1885–1973), who had also blended elements of Rinzai and Soto. Aitken studied with this Zen master as well. Aitken encountered Buddhism when he was sent to Japan as a World War II prisoner of war. Later, back in America, he studied with Nyogen Senzaki before meeting Yasutani. In 1959, Aitken set up the Diamond Sangha in Hawaii, and related centers emerged later. Aitken translated many Buddhist texts into English and fused the Western, liberal tradition of social action with Buddhism. His work also helped bring together representatives of the different Buddhist sects in America.

Another significant early convert was Jiyu Kennett (1924–1996). Originally from England, she met a Japanese Zen abbot in 1960, and two years later she was ordained a priest in Japan. Kennett was one of the first Western women to earn the title of *roshi*. In 1969, she came to the United States and soon after founded Shasta Abbey in California. Kennett also wrote about and taught Zen in North America and Europe. The organization she founded is now called the Order of Buddhist Contemplatives.

Kennett, Kapleau, and Aitken probably benefited from Beat Zen and Watts, who popularized Buddhism for the baby boomers. But even as they Americanized Zen in their centers, the Western *roshis*, their students, and other devoted converts represented a strong link to traditional Buddhist teachings.

The Vietnam War

Just as World War II gave some Americans their first direct contact with Buddhism, the Vietnam War boosted awareness of Buddhism in the United States. Hundreds of thousands of American soldiers fought in a country with strong Buddhist traditions, and some married Vietnamese women. The war also prompted many Vietnamese Buddhist monks to speak out against the corrupt government in South Vietnam—which received support from the United States—and to oppose the war in general.

In 1963, Americans were shocked to see television pictures of a man sitting cross-legged, on fire, in a South Vietnamese street. The man, a monk named Thu Vien Quang Duc, had set himself on fire to protest policies in South Vietnam. The suicide seemed to violate the Buddha's teachings against taking any life. Yet Buddhist masters said the suicide was just, since it served a higher good. Thich Thien An (1926–1980), a Vietnamese Buddhist who later came to America, said, (as quoted on www.tuvienquangduc.net/English/vnbuddhism/013 quangduc.html), "Accepting the most extreme suffering of his body, Thich Quang Duc burned himself and in so doing created the fire of

BUDDHIST TERMS OF RESPECT

The various Asian languages associated with Buddhism have different terms for the teachers and masters of the faith. In Tibetan, *rinpoche* mean "precious one." Zen Buddhists call their masters *roshi*—Japanese for "venerable (or honorable) teacher." Vietnamese Buddhist teachers often have *thich* in their name, which means "in the family of Buddha." Korean Zen masters are called *sunim*, which means "monk." Theravada monks and abbots are usually addressed with the English title "venerable."

consciousness and compassion in the hearts of the people." A few other monks and nuns also set themselves on fire during the Vietnam War. Although the suicides seemed bizarre to many Americans, they raised awareness about the situation in Vietnam and the nature of Buddhism.

Vietnamese Buddhist monks also used less extreme means to educate Americans about the war and their faith. Thich Nhat Hanh (b.1926) came to the United States in 1966, representing other monks who wanted to end the war. For Hanh, the conflict had a direct effect on his Buddhist beliefs. He later wrote in *Peace Is Every Step* (1992), "When I was in Vietnam, so many of our villages were being bombed . . . . I had to decide what to do. Should we continue to practice in our monasteries, or should we leave the meditation halls in order to help the people who were suffering under the bombs?"

Hanh's choice was to help the victims of the war—many suffering because of U.S. weapons. Hanh launched what he called "engaged Buddhism," and helped it develop in the West. As with Aitken's efforts at reform, engaged Buddhism appealed to Americans who wanted to use their Buddhist faith in an active way to change society, not just to seek individual enlightenment.

A Boost for Ethnic Buddhism

The United States government has often had a love-hate relationship with immigrants. At times, the country has welcomed the cheap, abundant labor immigrant workers provide. Other times, immigrants seem like a threat to jobs and American values—especially if the immigrants are thought to have "inferior" cultures or belong to a non-white race. The curbs on immigration enacted in 1924 kept out almost all Asian newcomers, limiting the growth of ethnic Buddhism.

In 1952, the United States loosened the restrictions on Asian immigration, but some limits remained. Finally, in 1965, Congress passed a new law that greatly increased immigration from Asia. Old, narrow quotas were scrapped, and priority was given to relatives of U.S. citizens, refugees, and people with professional skills. The increase in Asian immigration gave new life to Chinese Buddhist communities. It also led to the first large wave of Korean immigration.

After the Vietnam War, the U.S. government made special allowances for Southeast Asian refugees. The war affected Laos and Cambodia as well as Vietnam, and refugees came in great numbers from all

Changes in Immigration

The number of immigrants from Korea and China rose dramatically after the new immigration law went into effect in 1968. Here are the numbers of immigrants for some sample years:

	1965	1973	1986
Chinese *	4,769	21,656	43,571
Koreans	2,165	22,930	35,776

* mainland China, Hong Kong, Taiwan   Source: U.S. Immigration and Naturalization Service.

three countries. More than 500,000 refugees from those Southeast Asian nations entered the United States between 1981 and 1990. Another 30,000 came from Thailand. Except for Vietnam, these countries are primarily Theravada Buddhist, so the refugees helped create the first large-scale Theravadin presence in the United States. By 1996, the country had 142 Theravada temples, all but one built after 1970.

The Asian immigration boom continued during the 1990s. By 1999, about 10 percent of the foreign-born population in the United States came from China, Vietnam, and Korea, representing more than 2.5 million people. Although these immigrants and their American-born children worship in a variety of faiths, they represent a large pool of ethnic Buddhists.

The Tibetan Diaspora

A diaspora is the breaking up and scattering of the people of an ethnic community or nation. One of the first diasporas took place more than 2,500 years ago, when the Jewish people lost their independent state and began to settle in different parts of the Middle East and later in Europe. The dispersion of Africans because of the slave trade and the migration of the Irish after the potato famine of the 1840s have also been called diasporas.

As people scatter to different parts of the globe, they bring their religions with them. African slaves brought their beliefs to the New World, where these ideas sometimes blended with Christianity. The arrival of Irish immigrants in the United States tremendously boosted the strength of Roman Catholicism in the country. For American Buddhism, a significant diaspora started in 1959, when Tibet's Dalai Lama left his homeland.

Tibet had been an independent country for centuries when China invaded in 1950. Tucked in the Himalayas, Tibet was an isolated country ruled by its Buddhist lamas, following traditions that were centuries old. The Chinese declared that Tibet was a province of China, clamped down on the practice of Tibetan Buddhism, and ended the Dalai Lama's role as the political leader of Tibet. In 1959, fearing his life was in danger, the Dalai Lama escaped to India. A small-scale diaspora followed, as both monks and lay people fled to India and other neighboring countries. Once abroad, the Tibetans could openly practice their faith and try to regain their country's independence.

Tibetan Buddhism Flourishes

Even before 1959, Tibetan Buddhism had reached the United States. But the first major awareness of its teachings came during the 1970s. The first two teachers with wide appeal to American converts were Tarthang Tulku (b.1935) and Chogyam Trungpa (1939–1987). They helped popularize Tibetan practices in the West.

Tulku arrived in the United States in 1968 and settled in California. He belonged to the oldest Tibetan Buddhist tradition, Nyingma, which stressed meditation and tantric practices (see page 18). Tulku taught Americans, who then spread Nyingma teachings. He also started Dharma Publishing to publish his writings.

The Chinese have destroyed thousands of temples in Tibet, which housed many sacred books and works of art. In response, exiled Tibetans in the United States and American Vajrayana Buddhists have made a significant effort to translate Tibetan texts and write new works about Tibetan Buddhism in English.

Trungpa came to America in 1970, living in Vermont before ending up in Colorado. He represented the last of the four Tibetan orders to reach the United States, Kagyupa, although his teachings also have some Nyingma influence. Trungpa had studied in Great Britain and spoke fluent English. He eventually founded a Buddhist-influenced college, Colorado's Naropa Institute, and wrote several popular books. He also combined Buddhist teaching with other Eastern practices in what he called Shambhala. This practice, Trungpa wrote in *Shambhala: The Sacred Path of the Warrior* (1986), offered "secular enlightenment, that is, the possibility of uplifting our personal existence and that of others without the help of any religious outlook." Trungpa also came to represent a more flamboyant, Westernized Buddhist. Instead of wearing monk's robes and practicing self-denial, Trungpa, a former monk, wore Western clothes, smoked, and drank alcohol. He seemed less distant—if also less traditional—to Americans exploring Buddhism for the first time.

During the 1980s and the 1990s, the Dalai Lama visited the United States several times. His trips brought attention to the political repression still going on in Tibet. So did the work of celebrities interested in Tibetan Buddhism. Many promoted the Tibet issue, giving Tibetan Buddhism the popular attention Zen had received during the counterculture years of the 1960s.

Average Americans also embraced the monastic side of Tibetan Buddhism. The most famous of these converts might be Pema Chodron (b.1935), a nun born in America who now lives in Nova Scotia, Canada. She has written many books that bring Tibetan teachings to a wider audience.

Chodron, among others, has promoted *tonglen*, a meditative practice also called sending and receiving. In *tonglen*, the meditator breathes

Discovering Tulkus in America

In the Tibetan Buddhist tradition, *tulkus* are reincarnated lamas. They are identified by living lamas, and in Asia, *tulkus* are sometimes discovered when they are toddlers. With the development of Vajrayana in the United States, Tibetan lamas have declared that some native-born Americans are tulkus.

Around 1990, Jack Churchward of Florida was named a *tulku* when he was seven years old. His parents had studied Buddhism, and their sense that Jack was somehow "different" led them to Chetsang Rinpoche, who confirmed he was a *tulku*. At first Jack resisted taking on the responsibilities of a *tulku*, which included studying Buddhism at a monastery in India. Finally, in 2000, he changed his mind and was enthroned as the reincarnation of Tradak Tulku, who had run a Tibetan monastery a century before.

Jack went to India for two months of training, then returned to Florida. He plans to visit his own monastery in Tibet someday, but he also said he would like to keep his American roots. "If it's my choice," he told the *St. Petersburg Times* in a March 13, 2001, article. "I'd like to go back and forth."

Getting national press
The growing popularity of Buddhism and its place in American culture was demonstrated by this cover story in Time *magazine on October 13, 1997. Pictured is actor Brad Pitt, who starred in the Buddhist-themed movie* Seven Years in Tibet.

in negative forces from the world around them: hatred, suffering, and fear. These emotions are then converted into positive forces—love, health, strength—that are exhaled back to others.

The New Popular Buddhism

After the 1960s, convert Buddhism grew, thanks in large part to its appeal to artists and intellectuals. Although Zen, *vipassana*, and Tibetan traditions were the most common, Soka Gakkai also drew many new believers. Also, ethnic Buddhism skyrocketed due to immigration, although mainstream Americans might not have been aware this.

By the early 1990s, Buddhism was moving beyond the fringes of American society and receiving more attention. Buddhist scholarship increased at universities, and meditation centers—either strictly Buddhists or influenced by Buddhist practices—sprang up across the country. In 1987, Buddhist scholar Don Morreale published a guide to Buddhist meditation centers in North America, listing 429 centers. A revised edition published a decade later had more than 1,000 listings. Buddhists and the merely curious could also read about the dharma in two colorful magazines, *Tricycle* and *Shambhala Sun*.

One mark of Buddhism's growing acceptance was an October 13, 1997, cover article in *Time* magazine. With a circulation of more than 4 million, *Time* is the most popular news weekly in the country. Its coverage of Buddhism in America looked at the glitzy side of Buddhism—from Hollywood films that focused on Buddhism to a new make-up called "Zen blush." But the article also described the basics of Buddhist beliefs and interviewed Americans dedicated to the faith. These included Egyoku Nakao of Los Angeles. Of Japanese and Portuguese heritage, Nakao was the head priest at the Los Angeles Zen Center. Having a female head priest, the article noted, showed how Zen had changed since its arrival in America.

The article also pointed out that many convert Buddhists do not accept all the teachings of the faith, or give them less significance than traditional Buddhists do. *Time* talked to An Buck, who ran a Theravada meditation group out of her home. She was not as concerned with talking about karma as she was with filling "the enormous need of people to find a safe home, a refuge, within their being." Jack Kornfield, one of the founders of the insight meditation movement (see page 31), noted in the article that "American people don't want to be monks and nuns. They want practices that transform the heart."

Kornfield's statement applies to the many converts who come to Buddhism. It also applies to ethnic Buddhists seeking merit. In any faith, not all believers take the path to priesthood or monasticism. American Buddhism has a place for seekers at all levels, from the monks and nuns to the people merely looking to blend Buddhist teachings with other beliefs, or use them in a secular way for self-improvement.

3

Buddhism in American Culture

AS BUDDHISM SPREAD BEYOND ASIA, IT BLENDED WITH THE cultures of the new lands it entered. Buddhist beliefs mixed with native expressions of art, styles of education, and the daily attitudes and habits that shape a particular culture.

In the United States, Buddhism was and remains a key part of the cultural life for immigrants, as temple activities and festivals let new arrivals stay in touch with their ethnic roots. Each community's culture and Buddhist practices vary, reflecting the traditions of their different countries of origin. Through temple life, many Buddhist immigrants also had their first exposure to American culture, whether through learning English or picking up survival tips from previous arrivals.

Buddhism's impact on the larger, dominant culture—Anglo or European-American, a democratic, individualistic society traditionally dominated by white, Christian values—was minimal at first. From the founding of the North American colonies until the mid 1900s, Buddhism barely registered as a cultural force outside of ethnic Asian communities.

The larger cultural impact of Buddhism in America really began after World War II, when converts embraced Zen and other forms of Buddhism. Today, there is still something of a split between the more self-contained

Here is part of Elizabeth
Peabody's 1844 translation of
the Lotus Sutra.

*Full of water, surrounded
with a garland of lightning,
this great cloud [the Buddha],
which resounds with the
noise of thunder, spreads joy
over all creatures. Arresting
the rays of the sun, refreshing
the sphere of the world,
descending so near the earth
as to be touched with the
hand, it pours out water on
every side.*

PRECEDING PAGE
Buddhism in the movies
*Set in Tibet, but made by
American filmmaker Martin
Scorcese,* Kundun *told the
story of the young Dalai
Lama's growth and training.*

ethnic Buddhist culture and the broad role of Buddhism expressed in the dominant American culture. But as the two sides come together more on devotional practices, the two cultures start to overlap, as well.

Early Cultural Forces

For the first Chinese- and Japanese-American Buddhists, their religion was part of a larger cultural life that included festivals and celebrations tied to their homelands. As immigrants, however, most did not have time to express their Buddhism in art or literature; they were too busy trying to make a living in their new land. Monastic life traditionally gave rise to Buddhist art and writing, but the newcomers did not set up monasteries where those arts could flourish.

To native-born Americans of the 19th century, Asia was an exotic place, one that few North Americans visited. Wealthy travelers, missionaries, sea captains, and scholars were the exception, and some brought back Buddhist art. The religious traditions that inspired it, however, were not always a prime concern.

The Transcendentalists (see page 24), although influential among intellectuals, did not reach a wide popular audience. Still, they made the first efforts to bring Buddhism to public attention—at least as literature, if not as a widely practiced faith. In 1844, Ralph Waldo Emerson's literary magazine, *The Dial,* published the first known translation of a Buddhist text to appear in the United States. The selections from the Lotus Sutra were once thought to have been translated by Henry David Thoreau, the Transcendentalist writer best known for his book *Walden*. Instead, scholars learned in 1993 that the sutra had been translated by another Transcendentalist, Elizabeth Palmer Peabody (1804–1894). She worked from a French text that had been translated from Sanskrit a few years before.

The World's Parliament of Religions in 1893 (see page 25) did more than bring Buddhist teachers and doctrines to a wider American audience. Publisher Paul Carus, inspired by the Parliament, began creating art that promoted the Buddhist ideal. He wrote a play about the Buddha's life and wrote hymns on Buddhism that could be sung to modern Western music. Carus also wanted an Americanized version of the statues and paintings of the Buddha seen throughout Asia. Instead of the typical meditating Buddha, Carus said (as quoted in *The Faces of Buddhism in America*) Western art should show Buddha "in the various

Thoughtful American
Writer and philosopher Ralph Waldo Emerson was among those who helped bring Buddhist texts and ideas to Western audiences in the years before the Civil War.

phases of his life work." He thought an active Buddha with Western physical features would have more appeal to Americans.

Beat Art, Zen Art

The fascination of the Beats with Buddhism led them to introduce the dharma into their writings and to try to copy the Buddhist—specifically Zen—approach to art. For a Zen artist or writer, art is an expression of the human spirit at the moment the artwork is created. Spontaneous expression, done quickly, is more important than deep thoughts or complex forms.

Haiku is a form of Japanese poetry closely linked to Zen. The 17th century poet Basho (1644–1694), a master of haiku, studied Zen, and other Japanese haiku poets were Buddhist monks. In English, a haiku has three lines and a total of just 17 syllables—five in the first line, seven in the second, and five in the third. With just these few words, haiku poets quickly dive into the essence of their subject. The end result should provide, as Western scholar R. H. Blyth put it, "temporary enlightenment," as the reader grasps the poet's vision, while also adding his or her own experiences to the interpretation of the words.

Speaking of haiku in one of his essays, D.T. Suzuki wrote, "You do not have to compose a grand poem of many hundred lines to give vent to the feeling…awakened by looking into the abyss. When a feeling reaches its highest peak we remain silent, because no words are adequate. Even 17 syllables may be too many" (*Zen Buddhism*, 1956).

Jack Kerouac, Gary Snyder, and Allen Ginsberg all read about and practiced Buddhism. Kerouac's *The Dharma Bums*, published in 1958, follows the adventures of two young men interested in Buddhism as they travel across the West Coast. The book blends talk of the dharma with tales of sex and drugs. For many of the baby boomers who read it, *The Dharma Bums* offered them their first glimpse of Buddhist ideas, although in a form not found in any Asian monasteries.

Kerouac was also interested in haiku, and he changed the form slightly to create what he called American haiku pop. He stuck with three short lines, though not necessarily adding up to 17 syllables. The "pop" stood for the burst of enlightenment the poems were supposed to provide.

Zen Beyond Beat

Haiku, whether directly Buddhist or not, was known to American scholars during the late 19th and early 20th centuries. By the 1960s, it had worked its way into some elementary schools, as students studied Japanese culture and wrote their own haikus. The Buddhist-inspired writing of the Beats also found its way into the classroom, although at first many Americans found the references to sex and drugs offensive. Scholars now appreciate the role of Beat Zen in shaping the counterculture movement of the 1960s and beyond, and in bringing Buddhism to American culture.

The Zen influence in American culture went beyond Beat poetry and literature. After the Beats, other writers introduced Buddhism into their work. J.D. Salinger (b.1919) wrote a series of short stories during the early 1960s that featured Buddhist concepts. In the late 1970s, author Peter Matthiessen (b.1927) wrote *The Snow Leopard*, about his travels in Nepal, which reflected his growing interest in Zen. Matthiessen, who has also written several acclaimed novels, later was ordained as a Buddhist monk.

Visual arts in America were also influenced by Zen. In the Zen art style called *sumiye*, painters traditionally use a black ink made from

HAIKU BY BASHO

Here are some examples of haiku by Basho, written more than 300 years ago.

With dewdrops dripping,
I wish somehow I could wash
this perishing world

Tremble, oh my gravemound,
in time my cries will be
only this autumn wind

Even in Kyoto,
how I long for Kyoto
when the cuckoo sings

soot and glue. They apply the ink using a coarse brush made from sheep or badger's hair, making a quick sketch rather than a painting. Again, as with haiku, the idea is not to capture a detailed image, but to make a suggestion that might stimulate deeper awareness. In the United States, collectors bought original Japanese *sumiye* art, and some artists used the idea of spontaneity in their own brush-and-ink work.

During the 1970s and 1980s, Zen ideas were appearing in a number of books on subjects not directly related to Buddhism. Robert Pirsig wrote the best-seller *Zen and the Art of Motorcycle Maintenance* (1974), a book about the author's travels and his experiences on the road, as well as about Eastern and Western philosophy. *Zen and the Art of Archery* (1953) by Eugen Herrigel explored a German professor's six years studying Japanese archery. Western writers began to explore the Zen of many things, suggesting that such Buddhist concepts as mindfulness and emptiness could help people improve different parts of their lives. The books also explained how certain everyday activities or hobbies could be used as forms of meditation.

The explosion of Zen titles continued into the 1990s and the beginning of the 21st century. This growth reflected the continuing interest in Zen and Buddhism. It also may have reflected the belief among publishers that anything labeled "Zen" would attract more attention and sell more books, rather than a true interest in the dharma.

Another part of Japanese Zen culture transplanted to the United States is the dry garden. In these Zen gardens, white sand and rocks represent waves or streams of water. Larger rocks often sit in the middle of these sand oceans, which are raked to create the sense of moving water. The act of building the garden is seen as a form of active meditation, and then the garden is used as a meditation site.

As with many Zen principles, Zen gardens are sometimes built for their beauty or exotic nature, not to inspire Buddhist devotion. Mini table-top Zen gardens, complete with tiny rakes, would not seem to have the same impact as real gardens. Still, as more convert Buddhists appear, they appreciate the true purpose of the gardens and build them for that reason.

Musical Buddhism

Buddhism had less of an impact on American music than it did on literature, but Buddhist ideas still had some influence, and a number of

---

BUDDHISM IN POETRY

Here is a short excerpt from Gary Snyder's poem, *December at Yase*:

*I feel ancient, as though I had
Lived many lives.
And may never now know
If I am a fool
Or have done what my
     karma demands.*

These are two examples of Jack Kerouac's American haiku pop:

*The dog yawned
and almost swallowed
My Dharma*

*Missing a kick
at the icebox door
It closed anyway.*

musicians adopted Buddhist beliefs. After World War II, composer John Cage (1912–1992) was one of the many artists and intellectuals introduced to Zen through the lectures of D.T. Suzuki. Cage had already studied and written modern classical music when he began exploring Zen. Its ideas led him to develop what has been called "chance music"—musical expression done without formal notation or a planned approach to a composition. He would give musicians a bare outline of what to perform, letting the end result rest on chance and where the musicians felt themselves to be at that moment.

Cage also thought that silence could be a part of music. Musical pieces have often included rests or pauses, but Cage pushed the idea to extremes. His composition *4' 33"* has a musician sitting on stage for four minutes and 33 seconds of silence—a form of musical meditation for both the performer and the audience. During the premiere of *4' 33"* in 1952, the only sounds in the concert hall came from the wind and other natural sounds in and around the building—and the whispers of confused audience members.

Cage saw the value of the Buddhist notion of quieting the mind. He also realized that there was no such thing as silence, since nature, including the human body, constantly provides sounds—if people truly listened to them. Years after writing *4' 33"* and studying Buddhism he said, "I've thought of music as a means of changing the mind. I saw art not as something that consisted of a communication from the artist to an audience, but rather as an activity of sounds in which the artist found a way to let the sounds be themselves. And, in being themselves, to open the minds of people who made them or listened to them to other possibilities than they had previously considered." (Cage is quoted on www.azstarnet.com/~solo/4min33se.htm.)

Many people thought Cage's Buddhist-inspired work was meaningless or a deliberate attempt to upset them. Years later, however, critics and scholars appreciated his intent. In its summer 1992 issue, the Buddhist journal *Tricycle* wrote that Cage had done "as much to introduce a deliberately Buddhist view into the cultural discourse of the West as any artist alive."

Starting in the 1960s, the composer Philip Glass (b.1937) studied yoga and Buddhist meditation and applied what he learned to his approach to music. Glass's music has been called minimalist, with certain musical patterns repeated over and over. Some critics have called

THE ZEN BOOM

A look at a bookstore or library will turn up dozens of books that feature Zen in the title—some serious, some humorous. Many more books not focused on Zen reflect Buddhist attitudes. Some of the more interesting or unusual titles include *Zen and the Art of Stand-Up Comedy, Zen and the Art of Managing Up, Zen for Cats, The Art and Zen of Learning Golf,* and *Zen and the Art of Poker*.

it "meditation music," with the repeating pattern—marked by small changes over time—creating a hypnotic effect on the listener. Glass has also written operas, and he said he used these and other works to, as he told Tricycle.com (the online version of *Tricycle*), "reflect my feelings of social responsibility"—feelings shaped by his Tibetan Buddhist practice. Glass saw many parallels between the work of a musician and the teachings of dharma. Both require students to learn the basics, pay attention to details, and make an effort to improve. Buddhist artists often note how their meditative practices bolster their creative efforts.

Popular Music

By the 1970s, Buddhist ideas were entering popular music as well. For many young rock and roll fans, their first introduction to a Buddhist term may have been the song *Bodhisattva*, by Steely Dan. This 1973 song does not openly explore the dharma, but the narrator talks about selling his house and wanting to see the "shine of your Japan, the sparkle of your China."

Over time, some popular musicians adopted Buddhism in their lives, even if their beliefs are not directly expressed in their music. Jazz pianist Herbie Hancock (b.1940) and singer Tina Turner (b.1939) belong

Beastie Buddhist
Adam Yauch of the Beastie Boys, shown here accepting a 2001 MTV Music Video Award, is involved with Buddhism and has used some of its themes in his group's music.

to Soka Gakkai and practice Nichiren Buddhism. Hancock said in a 2002 television interview that he is drawn to Buddhism's "sense of re-examining conventional ways of doing things"—an important goal for many Buddhist artists. (You can read the interview on the Bravo TV web site, www.bravotv.com.) The impact of religion in Turner's life was clear in the 1993 biographical film *What's Love Got to Do With It*. Turner, played in the film by Angela Bassett, is seen chanting at her own small Buddhist altar.

Buddhism has also come to rap and punk music through Adam Yauch (b.1964) of the Beastie Boys. Yauch wrote a song called *Bodhisattva Vow* that restates the traditional vow in more modern terms. He has also taken the vow himself. During the 1993 Lollapalooza tour, he invited a group of Tibetan monks to tour with the band. Before each concert the monks performed Buddhist rituals and dances, giving hundreds of thousands of young Americans their first exposure to Buddhist culture.

The Hollywood Connection

Buddhism's most obvious impact on American culture may be through the movies. As early as the 1930s, Americans got a taste of Tibetan Buddhism in the film *Lost Horizon*. Although set in the mythical country of Shangri-La, the movie's locale was clearly based on Tibet, with long-robed monks living in a remote Himalayan monastery. *Lost Horizon*, however, did not deal with the dharma in any meaningful way.

During the 1990s, Hollywood finally began to show Buddhism in a more realistic way, influenced by the growth of the religion in America and a concern about the political situation in Tibet. The 1993 film *Little Buddha* told two stories: one about a young American boy found to be a *tulku*; the other a biography of Siddhartha Gautama. Dzongsar Khyentse (b.1960) served as an adviser on the film, and he told *Tricycle* in a Summer 1993 interview that movies are a powerful tool for spreading Buddhism. "This film is better than building a hundred monasteries because it will reach throughout the world."

In 1997, two movies set in Tibet reached U.S. movie theatres. *Seven Years in Tibet*, starring Brad Pitt, tells the story of Austrian Heinrich Harrer (b.1912), who converted to Buddhism while living in Tibet during the 1940s. *Kundun* is a biography of the early years of the Dalai Lama, up until his exile to India, featuring music composed by Philip

Glass. Directed by the highly respected Martin Scorsese, *Kundun* probably received the most attention in the media and brought a new awareness of Tibetan Buddhism.

Individual actors have embraced Buddhism, and although they may not make films on Buddhist subjects, they freely talk about their beliefs. The best known is Richard Gere (b.1949), who has starred in such hit films as *Pretty Woman* and *An Officer and a Gentleman*. A Buddhist since the late 1970s, Gere said during a June 7, 2002, interview published in *The Guardian* that he wants to "explore possibilities that always take me in the direction of wisdom." Other actors influenced by Buddhism include Sharon Stone (b.1958), Patrick Swayze (b.1954), and Willem Dafoe (b.1955).

Buddhism has also been the subject of independent films not made in Hollywood. Various documentaries have been made about Tibetan Buddhism and Buddhist communities in America. One film, *The Jew in the Lotus*, shows the connections between American Jews, Jewish converts (sometimes called JuBus), and Tibetan monks. The movie

Actor is a big supporter
Actor Richard Gere is among the most prominent American celebrities who support Buddhism and related causes. He has been particularly interested in Tibetan Buddhism.

For years, Steven Seagal (b.1952) was known as the star of action-packed martial arts films. Seagal also had an interested in Buddhism, nurtured by his study of the martial art aikido and several years spent in Japan. In 1997, Seagal was named a *tulku* by Penor Rinpoche (b.1932), head of the Nyingma tradition of Tibet.

The announcement raised some questions in the U.S. press, as both journalists and other Buddhists wondered how a star known for his violent roles could be a reincarnated lama. Penor Rinpoche addressed these concerns in a press release posted at his monastery's web site (and quoted in *Buddhism in America*, 1999), saying, "Any life condition can be used to serve beings and thus, from this point of view, it is possible to be both a popular movie star and a *tulku*." Shortly after his recognition as a *tulku*, Seagal told a television interviewer for the Public Broadcasting System, "The most important aspect of any religion should be human kindness. And to try to ease the suffering of others." (You can read this interview at the PBS Frontline web site, at www. pbs.org/wgbh/pages/frontline/shows/tibet/.)

was based on a book of the same name (written by Rodger Kamenetz and published in 1995), which points out the high percentage of Jewish Americans among convert Buddhists.

Another independent film to feature Buddhism was *The Cup* (1999). Dzongsar Khyentse followed his beliefs on the power of motion pictures to spread the dharma and made a movie about Tibetan monks obsessed with the World Cup international soccer tournament. The film received excellent reviews around the world, and its slow pace was compared to meditation.

The Influence of Tibet

Khyentse's film was part of a larger development of Tibetan Buddhist art in the United States. As more Tibetan exiles came to America, they introduced their traditional art forms. This art features elaborate, brightly colored paintings of Buddhas and other symbols of the religion. These artworks are used to help Buddhists in their visualization meditations. One type of painting is the *thangka*, or scroll painting, Done on cloth, these paintings are easily rolled up so lamas can carry them from one place to another.

Bells and prayer wheels are also part of Buddhist practice and expressions of creativity. Prayer wheels have metal cylinders attached to handles. Prayers are carved onto the cylinders or written on paper placed inside. Each turn of the wheel represents the reciting of the prayer and helps the user gain merit.

In the United States, the best-known form of Tibetan art is the sand painting. Lamas create mandalas out of sand. They carefully tap different colored sand out of small metal tubes into patterns they have memorized. The lamas believe that the mandalas can stop suffering and cure illness.

In an April 7, 2002 interview with the *Hartford Courant*, one lama said a sand mandala "helps people turn their thoughts to a more spiritual way." When the sand mandala is finished, the lamas sweep up the painting and pour the sand into a lake or stream. The entire process reflects the Buddhist notion that even the most beautiful and sacred art, like everything else in life, is impermanent.

Lamas have built and then destroyed sand mandalas at many museums and universities across America. Non-Buddhists and Buddhists alike come to watch the lamas create sand mandalas, while chanting fills the space. The scene tends to inspire calm and a sense of holiness, while also introducing Americans to important Buddhist values.

Buddhism in Sports

Sports and recreation are also expressions of a particular culture, and Buddhism has shaped those activities in both its native lands and the United States. In Japan, a form of archery called *kyudo* reflects Zen ideas of mindfulness and strict self-control. Japanese immigrants and curious Americans have brought *kyudo* to the United States, and many converts have come to appreciate Zen by taking up "the way of the bow." One *kyudo* master, Hideharu Onuma (1910–1990), said shooters "hope that the sharp sound of arrow penetrating paper will awaken us from the so-called 'dream of life' and give us real insight into the ultimate state of being." (You can read this interview at www.kyudo.com/kyudo-p.html)

Zen is also closely associated with several martial arts forms that are popular in America. These include aikido, karate, judo, and kendo. In each form, athletes combine physical activity with spiritual development. Many Americans who study these martial arts learn Buddhist ideas, even if they do not become practicing Buddhists. Many of the martial arts taught in the United States are modern forms of more ancient martial arts used by warriors such as the samurai in Japan. As with Zen, the arts stress the need for a student to work closely with a master.

JEWISH BUDDHISTS
Some studies suggest that about 15 percent of all American converts to Buddhism are Jewish, a much higher percentage than the total number of Jews in the U.S. population. Jewish-American culture has blended with Buddhism in the work of Allen Ginsberg, and several Jewish Buddhists were at the heart of the *vipassana* movement. Some of the earliest American converts were Jewish, including Julius Goldwater, who became a Jodo Shinshu priest in 1936.

Here today . . .
Working carefully and slowly, Tibetan monks here create a mandala made of sand. The intricate construction can take weeks to create, grain by grain, but when it is finished, it will be swept away to demonstrate the impermanence of all things.

Buddhism in athletics has moved beyond traditional Asian sports and is finding its way into Western games. As we have already mentioned, authors have tried to apply Zen attitudes and practices to golf, and Buddhist-inspired writers and athletes have looked at the possible value of Buddhist insight in other sports.

Perhaps the best-known Zen practitioner in the sports world is Phil Jackson (b.1945), coach of the Chicago Bulls and later the Los Angeles Lakers in the NBA. Jackson has often had his players meditate or practice yoga, and he recommends Buddhist books to influence their approach to the game. Some of the titles his players have read include *Zen Mind, Beginner's Mind* by Shunryu Suzuki (1904-1971), Jack Kerouac's *On the Road*, and *Siddhartha*, a novel about the Buddha by German author Hermann Hesse (1877–1962). Jackson has also written several books, including *Sacred Hoops*. "In basketball—as in life," he wrote in that book, "true joy comes from being fully present in each and every moment." Jackson's writings reflect a common occurrence in Buddhist-influenced culture in America: He blends Zen with other religious ideas, including Native American spiritual beliefs and Western philosophy.

Buddhism on the World Wide Web

Since the 1990s, the Internet has evolved as a significant part of American culture. Whether used for research, self-expression, or communication, the Internet and the World Wide Web have become tied to daily life. The Web is also an important tool for many American Buddhists, both converts and ethnic. It provides *sanghas* with a way to connect with members who cannot physically come to a temple or meditation hall. It also lets Buddhists easily share their beliefs with curious non-Buddhists or potential converts.

The growth of Web sites created by temples, Buddhist organizations, and individual Buddhists has led to what is called the "cybersangha." The term was first used by Gary Ray (b.1967), a Zen lay monk, in 1991. Ray realized that Buddhists in remote parts of the United States often lacked a real *sangha* they could be part of. The cybersangha, he said, ended that isolation. Ray and others created a site called Gassho that explores American Buddhism. By 2002, an organization called the Dharma Ring listed more than 200 Buddhist sites on the Web.

Ray, however, did not think the Internet could be the only source of Buddhist education and activity. He told *Conscious Living* in 1997, "At some point you've got to turn everything off and start doing some hard work." (You can read the whole interview at www.buddhanet.net/virtualb.htm.)

One prominent online Buddhist journal is the *Journal of Buddhist Ethics*, cofounded by American Buddhist scholars Charles Prebish and Damien Keown in 1994. This Web site (www.jbe.gold.ac.uk/) takes a more academic approach to the cybersangha, compared to sites maintained by monasteries, temples, and individual Buddhists. Topics include the early history of Buddhism, its development in Europe and North America, and its interaction with other faiths.

PRAYERS ON THE WIND

In Tibetan communities, brightly colored prayer flags often flutter outside homes and temples. The flags are called *lung ta* or "wind horse." Tibetan Buddhists believe the mantras written on the flags are carried on the wind, giving blessings to anyone who passes near them. In the United States, prayer flags are becoming more common among non-Tibetans, as people explore Buddhist traditions or honor the plight of Tibetan exiles.

Buddhism in American Society

IN TRADITIONAL ASIAN BUDDHISM, THE HIGHEST GOAL IS TO FOLLOW a monastic lifestyle as a way of reaching nirvana. For the laity, their goal is to live a compassionate, giving life, earning merit so they can achieve good karma—and hopefully reach enlightenment in a future life.

In the United States, the monastic ideal had often been downplayed, as both Asian masters and their students see how difficult it can be for fast-paced American lifestyles to mesh with monastic practice. Many Buddhist teachers look for ways to blend the practices and rules traditionally followed by monks with what most Americans would consider a regular lifestyle: holding a job, raising a family, engaging in a variety of social activities.

As a result, American Buddhism, especially among converts, has a growing public presence. As Helen Tworkov, editor of *Tricycle*, wrote in the Spring 1992 issue, American Buddhism "is out of robes, in the streets, in institutions, workplaces, and homes." Buddhist ideas influence health care, social relationships, and issues such as abortion and the death penalty. At the same time, traditional Buddhist culture confronts American values of equality and democracy, creating a Buddhist society different from the monastic-dominated one of Asia.

Engaged Buddhism

The first major effort to take Buddhism out of the monastery and into the larger society began during the Vietnam War. Thich Nhat Hanh and other monks at his Vietnamese monastery decided, as Hanh wrote in 1991, "to go out and help people and do so in mindfulness" (quoted in James William Coleman's 2001 book *The New Buddhism: The Western Transformation of an Ancient Tradition*). Hanh's desire to help others led to what he called socially engaged Buddhism (or just engaged Buddhism). In engaged Buddhism, Buddhists have an obligation to both pursue their own individual liberation from *samsara* and help others. Underlying this and similar efforts is the Mahayana belief in nonduality: there is no difference between one person and another, no boundaries created by race, gender, and wealth.

Hanh's ideas, through his lectures and books, found a receptive audience in the United States. (Many of his books were published by Parallax Press, which he helped found in 1985.) The country has always had a strong tradition of social reform, led by both churches and intellectuals. And Buddhism during the 1960s already appealed to many people who wanted to end the Vietnam War and solve such social ills as poverty and racism. Engaged Buddhism gave Americans a way to combine their social views with the dharma in a meaningful way.

Buddhist scholar Donald Rothberg has noted that engaged Buddhism usually follows one of two approaches. Some Buddhists pursue social action after first developing their own spiritual practice; the action is an expression of their understanding of the dharma. Others see the social action itself as a way to develop their Buddhist beliefs.

Engaged Buddhism in Action

Engaged Buddhism is expressed through various programs that try to end suffering in many different forms. One example is the Greyston Bakery, established in 1982 by Bernard Tetsugen Glassman (b.1939), a convert Zen priest. Glassman started the bakery as a way to raise money so Zen students could devote themselves to their monastic practices. As the bakery grew, it took on a larger social role.

Greyston provides jobs for unemployed people in its New York City neighborhood, and profits from the bakery fund programs that provide housing for the homeless, child care, and care for people suffering from HIV/AIDS.

The Buddhist Peace Fellowship (BPF) also has a wide-ranging focus on social issues, although its major focus is political (see page 76). In 1995, BPF started the Buddhist Alliance for Social Engagement (BASE). In BASE, participants work together for six months in such places as hospitals, soup kitchens, and prisons. At the same time, the group members study the dharma, deepening their commitment to Buddhism. Rothberg, who took part in BASE, wrote on the BPF Web site (www.bpf.org/basestor.html) that the group "met a deep longing felt by each of us, a longing to integrate the psychological, social, and spiritual dimensions of our lives."

Another Buddhist group with social goals is the Engaged Zen Foundation. The foundation was started to bring the dharma to prisoners and teach them zazen. (Other Buddhist groups have similar programs.) Over time, as its members saw the sometimes-harsh conditions in U.S. prisons, the Engaged Zen Foundation also began working for prison reform. It tries to make sure convicts receive proper treatment and their full legal rights. Members of the foundation oppose the death penalty.

Buddhism and Major Social Issues

The death penalty is just one social issue in the United States that attracts the attention of Buddhists. Most Americans favor the death penalty, but the Buddha's teachings lead to beliefs that sometimes come into conflict with dominant American opinions. Buddhists, following the teaching against harming any sentient being, oppose all forms of killing. That teaching also leads many Buddhists to become vegetarians, which puts them at odds with a dining culture largely based on eating meat and fish. Only about 3 percent of all Americans are vegetarians.

The Buddhist concern for all life forms has also led to the founding of several Buddhist environmental groups. Earth Sangha, based in Virginia, promotes "Buddhism in service to the Earth." The group relates its efforts to the first Bodhisattva vow: "Sentient beings are numberless, I vow to save them." A number of books in recent years have also made a connection between following the dharma and saving animal and plant life from human destruction.

Buddhists also have particular—if seemingly inconsistent—views on two other important social topics: abortion and euthanasia. Abortion brings up the moral teachings against killing, but Buddhists,

HOSPICE HELP

The Greyston Foundation is one of several Buddhist groups working with HIV/AIDS patients. Some of the best known are in California. They include the Zen Hospice Project in San Francisco and Maitri Hospice. The hospices provide a warm, caring atmosphere for people dying of AIDS. The Buddhist Peace Fellowship also runs the Buddhist AIDS Project, offering a wide range of information and services related to the disease.

like members of other American religious groups, disagree on whether a fetus is a person. Buddhists also might oppose the act of abortion, but still believe the choice to have one is up to each individual woman. And abortion may also play a karmic role. The child conceived by a man and a woman might have a karmic need not to achieve an incarnation at that time. Or perhaps the parents have their own karmic destiny that must be filled by conceiving yet not having a baby.

Many Buddhist teachers see abortion as a personal issue and advise students to meditate deeply before considering one. Some American Buddhist parents who opt for abortion follow a ritual done in Japan. Mizuko Kuyo is a service that honors the spirit of so-called "water babies"—aborted fetuses or children who die from miscarriages or during childbirth. Robert Aitken is one Zen priest who has performed this service for Americans. The ritual, Aitken wrote in an essay on ethics that was published in the Spring 1992 issue of *Tricycle*, lets parents find "that such basic changes [life and death] are relative waves on the great ocean of true nature, which is not born and does not pass away."

Euthanasia—killing someone who is close to death from a terminal disease—also seems to fall under the precept that forbids killing. But, as on many issues, Buddhism allows for shades of gray. In general, Buddhist teachers seem to oppose euthanasia. But some also oppose prolonging life with machines. Tibetan lama Dilgo Khyentse (1910–1991), in an essay that appeared in the Winter 1992 issue of *Tricycle*, said, "It is far better to let them die naturally in a peaceful atmosphere and perform positive actions on their behalf."

Challenge to Materialism

When the Pilgrims and Puritans of England reached what is now Massachusetts, they came looking for religious freedom. They also came for economic freedom. For them and other Protestants, success in business and material wealth were signs that God favored them and their efforts. For centuries, Americans have been encouraged to follow this "Protestant work ethic": work hard, take risks in business, and enjoy the results of that labor.

By the late 1800s, however, some Americans saw this work ethic turning into materialism. The religious element of the ethic, which limited the tendency to flaunt wealth or use it improperly, gave way to what 19th century scholar Thorstein Veblen (1857–1929) called "conspicuous consumption." Americans bought goods to show off their wealth and compete with their neighbors to have the biggest and best of everything. During the 20th century, the United States developed a consumer culture. People were encouraged to buy more goods, borrowing money if necessary. Advertising urged them that they needed the latest and greatest of any product.

Buddhism began attracting converts in America at a time when the consumer culture was booming. Buddhism appealed to people who felt materialism was a problem. But in the larger American society, the Buddhist message competes against a culture that either does not think much about consumerism, or relies on it for economic survival. Many engaged Buddhists see a need to challenge the acceptance of materialism and consumerism in American society.

The Buddha said, "Greed is the worst of afflictions"; yet Buddhism does not necessarily condemn wealthy people, as long as they obtain their wealth honestly. The rich who use their wealth for good ends and are not attached to their belongings can still be good Buddhists.

To many socially engaged Buddhists, however, the American consumer culture is a negative influence that keeps people from finding their Buddhahood. As an essay at the Buddhist Peace Fellowship web site (www.bpf.org) puts it, "The basic problem, however, is that consumerism doesn't work and can't work, in the deepest and most important sense—as a way to give our lives satisfactory meaning." This message is often repeated by American Buddhists who want to help others find enlightenment.

Buddhists realize that people cannot stop buying things: they need food, clothing, tools, and items that promote learning and recreation. But American Buddhists want to weaken the effects of consumerism, and show how greed and craving are at the root of suffering. Engaged Buddhists also encourage people to be mindful when they shop. Certain goods are produced in horrible conditions around the world. A mindful shopper buys items that caused the least suffering to people and the environment as they were made.

Medical Buddhism

Since the 1970s, many convert Buddhists and Americans influenced by Buddhism have seen the role meditation and mindfulness can play in promoting good health. One of the pioneers of this approach is Jon

Freud meets Buddha
Psychiatrist Mark Epstein (left) and insight meditation teacher Joseph Goldstein explored the meeting of Buddhist and Western psychologies during this 2001 lecture.

Kabat-Zinn. Kabat-Zinn, who has a Ph.D. in molecular biology, studied yoga along with Zen and Theravada Buddhism. He devised a meditation practice that could be used to help reduce stress and chronic pain. Kabat-Zinn set up the Stress Reduction Clinic at the University of Massachusetts medical center and wrote and lectured on his work. His program has been copied around the United States.

Kabat-Zinn, like Thich Nhat Hanh and others, stresses the need to be mindful in daily activities. Washing dishes or making the bed can be Buddhist activities, if a person focuses only on those actions and does not let stray thoughts and worries cloud the brain. Kabat-Zinn and others using his meditation methods are not necessarily interested in the religion of Buddhism. Instead, they want to apply some of its teaching to everyday life, as a way to promote better health.

"Although I teach Buddhist meditation," Kabat-Zinn said at a conference in 1997 (as quoted in Richard Hughes Seager's 1999 book, *Buddhism in America*), "...it's not with the aim of people becoming Buddhists, but with the aim of them realizing that they are Buddhas. And there's a huge distinction."

American Buddhists have also seen that Buddhism can be important for mental health. Decades ago, prominent psychotherapists Carl Jung (1885–1961) and Erich Fromm (1900–1980) noted that Zen could play a role in helping people with psychological problems. The connection between therapy and Buddhism in all its forms has deepened since the 1970s.

The bridging of the two worlds usually comes from therapists trained in Western psychotherapy who are exploring Buddhism, as opposed to devoted Buddhists embracing therapy. Ryo Imamura (b.1944), however, is an exception. He comes from a long line of Jodo Shinshu priests, yet also studied psychotherapy. He has rare insights into both realms, those of ethnic and convert Buddhists. Imamura wrote in an essay published in *The Faces of Buddhism in America* that many Westerners he meets "regard the temple to be a kind of therapy center and the Buddhist priest to be a type of psychotherapist." That notion, he noted, would be foreign to the Japanese Americans who come to his temple. Imamura also sees limits in trying to use Buddhism as therapy, without truly understanding the dharma or joining a *sangha*.

Some convert therapists, however, believe Buddhist teachings can be useful in improving mental happiness, even if they do not lead to nirvana. Mark Epstein (b.1953) is a psychiatrist and practicing Buddhist. He studied all the traditional Western approaches to therapy while also exploring meditation and the dharma. He finally concluded that the Western notions of the ego and the self, and making that self healthy and happy, were limited. As Epstein wrote in *Going to Pieces Without Falling Apart* (1998), "In Buddhism, the impenetrable, separate and individuated self is more of the problem than the solution." Epstein and other therapists have tried to help patients by introducing them to meditation or focusing on issues beyond making the self happy, such as the ultimate nature of reality. Patients do not have to accept Buddhism as their religion to benefit from the insights it can offer about human existence.

Getting Along in a Diverse Society

Throughout the history of the United States, certain groups have faced legal discrimination or physical violence because of their race, religion, or ethnic background. As Buddhism has grown in America, its followers have played a role in bridging the gap between different social groups. Yet within the various schools of Buddhism, practitioners still see social divisions. Some are rooted in traditional Buddhist attitudes, while others reflect American prejudices.

Buddhists are taught to show compassion to others and realize that everyone is connected. These ideas lead many American Buddhists to work for social justice and against poverty. In the United States, African Americans and other minorities have often been victims of injustice and poverty. The social goals of Buddhism would seem to make it attractive to these groups. Yet converts to Buddhism are almost exclusively white, with one major exception.

Soka Gakkai has actively taken its form of Nichiren Buddhism into traditionally black and Hispanic neighborhoods. Its message of chanting to bring about self-improvement met with a receptive audience. So did the Buddhist notion that humans are responsible for their own fate, through their karma. By one estimate, blacks and Hispanics make up almost 30 percent of Soka Gakkai's American membership. But in general, non-Asian minorities have been slow to embrace Buddhism. African-American author, scholar, and Buddhist bell hooks (b.1952) told *Tricycle* in the Fall 1992 issue, "many people see the contemplative traditions—specifically those from Asia—as being for privileged white people."

Despite that attitude, more African Americans are discovering Buddhism. There is a history of blacks looking to the East for inspiration, as outlined by African-American novelist and Buddhist Charles Johnson (b.1948). He noted that civil rights leader Martin Luther King Jr. was inspired by Asian attitudes on non-violence. King also described the interconnection of all people in a way that echoes Buddhist teachings, and during the 1960s, he nominated Thich Nhat Hanh for the Nobel Peace Prize.

But other black Buddhists have pointed out that some members of their community still feel out of place or discriminated against in mostly white *sanghas*. In response, some saw the need for exclusively black Buddhist communities. Lewis Woods, a follower of *vipassana*, made this suggestion in 1996. Woods, however, hoped it would be a temporary arrangement, until there was better understanding between white and black converts.

African-American Buddhists from different traditions have also begun to talk with one another. In 2002, the Spirit Rock Meditation Cen-

Three Buddhists in One
Bhante Suhita Dharma is a rarity among American Buddhists, black, white, or Asian. Trained as a Roman Catholic monk, he eventually became the first African American to be ordained a monk in the three major Buddhist vehicles. He studied most closely with Thich Thien An. The Rev. Suhita has worked with AIDS patients and the homeless in both California and New York.

ter of California held the first major gathering of black dharma teachers from all the major forms of Buddhism.

Just as the convert community sometimes splits along racial lines, the overall convert community is still largely separated from the ethnic Buddhist community. Buddhist scholar Rick Fields has studied this split. He says many converts learn their Buddhism from Asians, either in the United States or abroad. But in their religious practice, the converts are cut off from the ethnic communities. The temple services are often held in Asian languages, leaving out converts who have not studied them. And for some converts, the rituals in a temple remind them of the Western religious practices they wanted to escape by embracing Buddhism.

Kenneth Tanaka has studied the split from the Asian perspective. In 1998, he surveyed members of various Asian temples near San Francisco. Most said they knew only a few convert Buddhists personally, and about half could not name any prominent non-Asian Buddhists. Those who could usually named actor Richard Gere. Tanaka also noted that even Asian Buddhists from a particular country, such as Korea or

Taiwan, had little contact with Asian-American Buddhists from other ethnic backgrounds.

Still, both Tanaka and Fields believe there is a growing effort to bridge the two communities. Tanaka found that ethnic Buddhists are eager to have non-Asians join their temples. And Fields believes American convert Buddhism can be enriched by certain Asian traditions. At the heart of Pure Land Buddhism is the idea of gratitude, of giving thanks every day. "This attitude of thankfulness or gratitude," Fields wrote in *The Faces of Buddhism in America*, "provides a valuable addition to the enlightenment-seeking tendencies of white Buddhism."

Sex and Sexism

In the United States, Buddhists have often discussed the role of women in Buddhism, as well as the issue of homosexuality. Traditionally, Asian Buddhist communities have been dominated by men, although nuns have often played an important role. In the United States, only a few converts have become nuns; the first ordinations did not take place until 1988. Most female Buddhists remain in the laity, but they refuse to accept a second-class role.

Some write about Buddhism through a woman's perspective. One well-known book is *Opening the Lotus: A Women's Guide to Buddhism* (1998), by Sandy Boucher. She blends feminism and Buddhism, although not all female Buddhists follow feminist beliefs. Boucher also lists female teachers. More women have become teachers since the 1970s, but the process has been slow. Most of the Asian teachers who have come to the United States are men. They tend to have traditional ideas about the role of women in Buddhism and society. At first, they often gave transmission (passed on their teachings) only to other men. However, nuns and female priests are now playing prominent roles in some *sanghas* and in bringing the dharma to society at large.

Within a *sangha*, the master or lama is the ultimate authority. At times, that power can be used in destructive ways. During the 1980s and early 1990s, several American Buddhists centers were shaken by controversy, as students charged their teachers with sexual abuse. Some centers set up rules to govern relations between students and teachers. There was a larger impulse to bring equality and democracy into the *sangha*. At the same time, the Buddhist tradition stressed the importance of students learning from masters. Buddhist scholars have noted a tension between American ideas about equality and that traditional authoritarian relationship.

One landmark study of Buddhism and feminism appeared in 1993. In *Buddhism After Patriarchy*, Rita Gross pointed out that Buddhism developed in lands where men controlled society. That impulse remained in the Buddhism brought to the United States. But Gross also noted that Buddhism is not, at root, tied to a god seen as an all-knowing father figure. The message of the dharma applies equally to men and women. And historical Buddhism has many strong female figures women can relate to, starting with Kuan Yin (see page 15).

In later writings, Gross has argued that merely having women receiving transmission is not enough to guarantee equality. "Unfortunately, in many systems, the first women to achieve authority are clones of the men who have always held authority, which solves almost nothing," she is quoted in *The Faces of Buddhism in America*. The key, she says is having women with feminist beliefs taking roles of authority in the United States. But since not all women accept feminism, there is not total agreement on this need.

Some Buddhists are also split over the place of gays and lesbians within their faith. Buddhist teachings are not clear about same-sex relations; the Third Precept regarding sexual activity can be interpreted many ways. Other ancient Buddhist texts, however seem to come down against homosexuality, although in general Buddhism is not actively against it. Roger Corless, a gay Buddhist scholar, notes that he has rarely heard anti-gay feelings among Buddhist teachers in the United States.

Some *sanghas* have been formed specifically to serve the religious needs of gay and lesbian Buddhists. One, based in San Francisco, is the Gay Buddhist Fellowship. Soka Gokkai is one form of Buddhism that seems to attract a large number of gays and lesbians. It performs same-sex marriages and has a history of being open to members of alienated groups.

5

Buddhism in American Politics

THE BUDDHA WAS A GREAT PRINCE, BUT MANY OF HIS EARLY followers were simple commoners. Just as with Christianity, Buddhism had great appeal among people who lacked political and economic power. But over time, as with Christianity, great rulers embraced the Buddha's teachings and spread it throughout their lands. Some, like Ashoka of India (see page 13), even carried the dharma far beyond the borders of their own countries.

Over the centuries, various Asian rulers relied on Buddhist monks to serve in their court, as diplomats and scholars. Some kings, such as Thailand's King Rama IV (1804–1868), lived as monks before taking the throne. Asian political history was shaped by the influence of Buddhism, and its role continues today, as Buddhist groups in different Asian countries work for democracy and peace.

In the United States, the political impact of Buddhism has been slight, at least until the latest spurt of convert Buddhism at the end of the 20th century. The first ethnic Buddhists faced discrimination and were not part of mainstream politics. Most Asian immigrants could not become citizens, and thus could not vote, until 1952. (Their children born in the United States automatically became U.S. citizens after the passage of the 14th Amendment to the Constitution in 1868.) Even white European immigrants who were not

PRECEDING PAGE

Praying for peace
Buddhist monk Takako Ichika Wa prays at the entrance to the Nevada Nuclear Test Site Area in Mercury, Nevada, during a protest in May 2000. Peace issues are a key Buddhist political focus.

Protestants have had trouble entering the upper levels of American political society. Only one Catholic, John F. Kennedy, has ever served as president, and only one Jew, Joseph Lieberman, has run for vice president or president. Still, the growing Buddhist community takes an active interest in certain political issues. As with social problems, politically inclined Buddhists build on the teachings that stress compassion and the oneness of all people.

Engaged Buddhists

The interest in bringing Buddhism into American politics is another expression of engaged Buddhism (see chapter 4) . The desire to move out of the meditation hall or temple and bring Buddhist teachings into everyday life affects both social and political issues. Many times, politics is a tool for making important social changes.

American Buddhists tend to be liberal when it comes to U.S. politics. They are often willing to use the powers of the federal government to help the needy, protect the environment, and limit the influence of the wealthy. Buddhists in politics also tend to be heavily influenced by the First Precept—take no life—and are active in the peace movement.

Just as individual meditation and Buddhist practice can prepare people to take on larger social issues, they are also important for political activists. Kenneth Kraft (b.1949), a Buddhist scholar and a follower of engaged Buddhism, thinks meditation is more about the process than about reaching a goal. "That approach is valuable in politics," Kraft said in a 2000 interview with *Interfaith Insights* (you can read the interview at www.interfaithinsights.org/00fa/kraft.html), "because often we don't see the immediate fruits of action. One can learn to work joyously, even without visible results, by appreciating the work of the moment."

Political action for American Buddhists usually comes at the local level or through organizations. U.S. Buddhists are not likely to actually run for public office. As of 2000, the U.S. Congress had no Buddhist members, although perhaps some have been influenced by Buddhist thought or share Buddhist political goals.

The Buddhist Vision at Work

In the national arena, one American politician with an interest in Buddhism is Jerry Brown (b.1938). Once the governor of California and a presidential candidate, Brown was elected mayor of Oakland, California, in 1998. Brown studied to become a Roman Catholic monk before entering politics. Later in life, he traveled to Japan to study Zen, and Buddhist ideas have influenced in his approach to governing.

Most politics, brown has said, is based on manipulating voters and creating illusions. The aim of Buddhism is to cut through illusions. "As a political leader," Brown said during a 1999 interview with *Grace Online* (www.gracecathedral.org/enrichment/interviews/int_19991029.shtml), "I strive for clarity. And if I could add the other dimension, it's caring. Caring and clarity." Brown's efforts in Oakland have included promoting environmental issues and stirring economic growth in a city that has often had a high level of poverty.

Since the early 1990s, Robert Thurman (b.1941) has actively tried to create a Buddhist-inspired "platform" for American politics. Before the 1992 presidential election, he explained in the Fall 1992 issue of *Tricycle* that Buddhist and American values are similar. "People should stop thinking that Buddhism is something weird and strange," he said. "Buddhist insight provides powerful support for…enlightened individualism." That individualism, Thurman said, includes such things as liberty, equality, and personal power. In other writings, Thurman stressed that political Buddhism, as he sees it, promotes the rights of minority groups and opposes racism in all its forms.

Kenneth Kraft has also looked at what issues and values should inform American Buddhist politics. He sees the Five Precepts (see page 12) as the foundation, just as Jewish and Christian politicians might use the 10 Commandments to shape their beliefs and actions. Kraft also looks to the Eightfold Path (see page 12) and its call for right speech—to speak truthfully and with no intent to harm others. "If that principle could be brought into the political realm," he said in an online interview (www.interfaithinsights.org/00fa/kraft.html), "it would certainly raise the level of political discourse."

Buddhism and the Peace Movement

During the Cold War of the last half of 20th century, the United States and the Soviet Union competed globally to spread their influence and different political systems—capitalism and democracy versus communism. Both sides built a huge arsenal of nuclear weapons, along with conventional forces. By the late 1970s, several American Buddhists

WHEN POLITICS AND RELIGION DO NOT MIX

Many Americans who are not really aware of Buddhism might have gotten their first exposure to it during the 1996 presidential campaign. Unfortunately, a highly publicized fund-raising incident did not reflect well on the religion's involvement in U.S. politics. Vice President Al Gore visited the Hsi Lai temple in Los Angeles, the largest Buddhist monastery in the country. Gore got into trouble for saying his visit was not a fundraiser, when actually it was. The temple also broke election laws by paying back monks and nuns for donations they made to Gore's campaign. The incident also raised the question of whether Master Hsing Yun (b.1926), founder of the temple, was trying to influence U.S. policy toward Taiwan, where he had once lived.

felt they needed to work against the build-up of nuclear arms and promote peace.

In 1978, Robert Aitken and several friends started the Buddhist Peace Fellowship (BPF). Aitken and others hoped to combine the peace movement that grew during the 1960s to protest the Vietnam War with a Buddhist approach. "I thought it was time to move out from under the Bodhi Tree, that our habitat and our life were in danger from nuclear weapons," Aitken said in a Spring 1993 interview in *Tricycle*. Other key early members of BPF included Gary Snyder and Joanna Macy (b.1929), who are still involved with the group.

The BPF drew inspiration from Thich Nhat Hanh and his efforts with engaged Buddhism (see page 62). He made several visits to the United States during the 1980s that helped boost interest in the fellowship and gave a new focus to American Buddhism. Andy Cooper, a former board member of BPF, told *Tricycle* in the Spring 1993 issue, "Before BPF, political work was seen as a distraction from dharma, essentially associated with confusion and bitterness. Now the issue of social and political involvement is central to the whole way we talk about Buddhism today."

Marching for peace
Members of the Buddhist peace fellowship march in San Francisco in late 2001 in protest of American military action following the September 11 terrorist attacks on the United States.

BPF's Issues Today

BPF started primarily as a convert movement, but it has worked to bring Asian Buddhists into its leadership and embrace all the Buddhist traditions. Today BPF has more than 15 chapters across the United States. Its members and related groups tackle political and social issues around the world, promoting democracy and human rights. Its international efforts included working for the release of Aung San Suu Kyi (b.1945), a Burmese peace activist and political reformer. Suu Kyi, a Buddhist, won the Nobel Peace Prize 1991 while under arrest for her political activities. She was released, rearrested, and finally released again in 2002.

In the United States, BPF protested the arms race fueled by the Cold War. BPF members blocked the shipment of weapons and called for an end to nuclear arms. Today, it tries to limit the spread of land mines and calls attention to violence committed in the United States using cheap handguns.

BPF members also take an interest in economic issues. Past BPF director Alan Senauke was one of several members who took part in international discussions on how to end poverty through economic and political programs. At the 1999 World Trade Organization meeting, held in Seattle, Washington, BPF members joined protests against the power of large international companies—many based in the United States—in the world's economy.

Think Sangha, the BPF's think tank on social and political issues, featured an essay by David Loy on these transnational organizations. He wrote, "Despite the talk we occasionally hear about 'enlightened' corporations, a corporation cannot become enlightened in the spiritual sense"—because a corporation is not like a person who can identify him or herself with the rest of the universe. Loy warned that "increasingly, the destiny of the earth is in the hands of impersonal institutions which, because of the way they are structured, are motivated not by concern for the well-being of the earth's inhabitants but by desire for their own growth and profit." (You can read Loy's essay at www.bpf.org/loy-corp.html.)

The BPF took a particular interest in the September 11, 2001, terrorist attacks on New York and Washington, D.C., and the response to them. Many Americans supported sending U.S. troops to Afghanistan and giving the U.S. government more powers to prevent any future attacks. The BPF kept promoting its message of peace while trying to help people understand what causes terrorists and other foreigners to feel such hatred for the United States. In the Winter 2002 issue of the BPF magazine *Turning Wheel*, Rosa Zubizarreta wrote, "As Buddhists, we hold to the truth that 'hate does not cease by hate, but by love alone.'" The BPF also brought up the notion that nations, like people, have karma. According to this idea, past actions by the American people, through their government, played a part in the tragedy of September 11, although many Americans did not appreciate this sentiment. Still, despite its sometimes-unpopular positions, BPF reported an increase in membership after September 11, as people opposed to war felt a need to work with others who held the same values.

Tibet and American Politics

War and violence are at the heart of another political issue that concerns many American Buddhists: Tibet. The Chinese takeover of Tibet brought Vajrayana Buddhism to the world's attention, as Tibetans fled their homeland for India, Nepal, and then North America and Europe.

Meeting of the minds

As an internationally respected religious leader, the Dalai Lama often meets with heads of state, such as here in 1999 with President Bill Clinton. The Dalai Lama lives in exile from his home country of Tibet, which was taken over by China.

In Tibet, before the Chinese takeover, politics and religion were united. Tibet was a theocracy, a country ruled by its religious leader—in this case, the Dalai Lama.

The exile of the Dalai Lama and other Tibetan lamas gave many Americans the chance to study Tibetan Buddhism: The current Dalai Lama, on his trips to the United States, has both taught the dharma and called attention to political strife in his homeland. It also led these Buddhists to ask the United States to become politically involved in Tibet's fight for independence. Prominent American Buddhists, such as actor Richard Gere, have joined this cause. At the 1993 Academy Awards, Gere asked the audience to send "love and truth" to Chinese leaders so they would remove their troops from Tibet. Gere also started the Gere Foundation, which donates money to the Dalai Lama and various Tibetan organizations.

Gere told the news show *Frontline* in 1997 that working for Tibetan independence is both a political issue and a religious one: "All the work that all of us have done in the West to help Tibetan culture is ultimately been about our own transcendence, no question about it. And in saving Tibet you save the possibility that we are all brothers [and] sisters." (This interview is found at the same link as noted in the sidebar on page 56.)

The telling of Tibet's story in films and the spread of its art in America—sand mandalas, chanting, folk art—have a political element, as well as reflecting the country's Buddhist heritage (see chapter 4). The study or presentation of Tibetan culture almost always leads to exploring the issue of Chinese domination.

Non-Buddhists and Buddhists Working Together

Tibet has presented a delicate issue for U.S. politicians. Some members of Congress oppose China's policies in general, not just in Tibet. The country denies its citizens free speech and the free practice of any religion. On the other hand, many politicians and business leaders want to trade with China. Bringing up Tibet or other difficult issues angers the Chinese and creates tensions between the two nations.

Tibetan Buddhists and American converts try to bring the larger American population to their way of thinking, despite the effects it might have on Chinese-American relations. To Tibet's American supporters, the issue is about freedom and human rights—values most Americans say they cherish.

Buddhists are having increasing success in winning support for their cause. In some cases, politicians with varied philosophies—liberal, moderate, and conservative—unite on this one issue. In 2002, the U.S. Senate passed a resolution calling for China to free the Panchen Lama, who was held by the Chinese. The Panchen Lama is second only to the Dalai Lama as a leader of Tibetan Buddhism. The Senate noted that other Tibetan political prisoners had been freed thanks to efforts by the U.S. government.

Also in 2002 in the House of Representatives, 42 members submitted a resolution calling on the U.S. government to "give serious consideration to recognizing the authorities of Tibet who are currently exiled in Dharamsala, India [including the Dalai Lama], as the legitimate representatives of Tibet." Nancy Pelosi, a Democrat from California, was one of the leaders on this issue. She met with Chinese vice president Hu Jintao in April 2002 and tried to deliver letters from other representatives expressing their views on Tibet. Hu refused to accept

THE MILAREPA FUND

Adam Yauch of the Beastie Boys has organized several benefit concerts that raise money for Tibetan exiles. He also started the Milarepa Fund to help Tibetans regain their independence through non-violent means. The fund is named for a Tibetan Buddhist poet who is often called a "saint" of Vajrayana.

them. As quoted at the International Campaign for Tibet Web site (www.savetibet.org/News/News.cfm?ID=1009&c=6), Pelosi said, "I had been hopeful that we could at least talk about human rights issues in China and Tibet, but Vice President Hu's refusal demonstrates how serious the problem remains."

Early U.S. Interest in Tibet

Newsweek magazine, in the April 19, 1999, issue, revealed that the U.S. government had tried to help the Dalai Lama and Tibetans long before American Buddhists took up the issue. During the 1950s, the Central Intelligence Agency (CIA) trained some Tibetans to work as spies and guerrilla fighters against the Chinese. The Tibetans parachuted from unmarked U.S. planes into their homeland. Most of these freedom fighters were killed or captured, but their spy efforts did uncover important information for the CIA. The Dalai Lama has also written about this American involvement in Tibet in his autobiography, *Freedom in Exile* (1990). In the *Newsweek* article, he called the effort a "sad, sad story," since the loss of the guerrillas did not lead to Tibet's freedom.

Leading Figures in American Buddhism

THE PEOPLE WHO HAVE SHAPED AMERICAN BUDDHISM COME FROM a variety of backgrounds and define their religion in different ways. All, however, believe in the power of Buddha's teachings to end suffering and the wheel of life and death. Here are just some of the more important American Buddhists of the past two centuries.

Dwight Goddard (1861–1939)

Almost forgotten today, Dwight Goddard gave many early convert Buddhists their first exposure to Buddhist texts. As Goddard wrote in the preface to his *A Buddhist Bible*, Buddhism is "the most promising of all the great religions to meet the problems of European civilization, which to thinking people are increasingly foreboding."

Goddard was born in Worcester, Massachusetts, and studied engineering before becoming a Baptist minister and missionary. His religious service took him to China, where he first learned about Buddhism.

Returning to the United States around 1899, Goddard soon gave up the ministry to enter business. After making a fortune as an inventor, he retired and returned to spiritual matters. During several trips back to China, Goddard continued to study Buddhism. Then in 1928, while in New York, he encountered Zen for the first time. Returning to Asia, he studied Zen in Japan, meeting D. T. Suzuki during his trip.

In 1932, Goddard published the first edition of his *A Buddhist Bible*. It was the first work to offer an English translation of Mahayana, Theravada, and Tibetan writings in one book. Goddard's "bible" is best known today as the source that inspired Beat writer Jack Kerouac to embrace Buddhism. The book is still in print.

Goddard also tried to start a monastic tradition for American converts. In 1934 he started the Followers of Buddha and planned to set up monasteries in California and Vermont. Lack of members ended Goddard's plan.

Yemyo Imamura (1867–1932)

The roots of ethnic Buddhism in the United States go back to the first Asian communities established in Hawaii. Several notable Japanese priests played a role in promoting Buddhism on the islands before they became part of the United States. One of the most important was Yemyo Imamura.

Imamura was born in Japan and was named a Jodo Shinshu Buddhist missionary to Hawaii in 1899. The next year, he became bishop of the Honpa Hongwanji Mission, a position he held for the rest of his life. Imamura wanted to Americanize Buddhism in Hawaii. He set up schools that taught Japanese children English and helped them learn good citizenship. The temple he built reflected Indian rather than Japanese architecture; Imamura wanted to emphasize Buddhism's native country and not stress the Japanese nature of Shinshu. Imamura was also an early engaged Buddhist: He tried to improve conditions for Hawaii's sugar workers, and during World War I he spoke out against the war. His grandson, Ryo Imamura, is a Buddhist priest and scholar.

D. T. Suzuki (1870–1966)

Daisetz Teitaro Suzuki was 27 when he first arrived in the United States. At the request of his Zen master, Soyen Shaku, Suzuki came to help spread Zen in America. Throughout the rest of his life, Suzuki did more than any other single person to educate Americans about the philosophy of Zen.

Born in Kanazawa, Japan, Suzuki began studying with Shaku as a college student. Unlike most prominent Asian Buddhists who came

PRECEDING PAGE
Zen master
Writer and teacher D. T. Suzuki was the primary force behind the introduction and spread of Zen Buddhism in the United States.

to America, Suzuki never received ordination as a monk. He did, however, experience *satori*—the Japanese word for enlightenment—while working on a famous Zen koan. Suzuki's focus was on the academic study of Buddhism, both Zen and Shin. He wrote many books that were translated from Japanese into English, and he also translated Asian texts for Western readers.

In 1897, Suzuki began working with American publisher Paul Carus. He also served as Shaku's translator when the Zen master toured the United States in 1905–1906. In 1911, Suzuki married an American, Beatrice Lane—a follower of the Theosophist teachings of Helena Blavatsky, which were heavily influenced by Buddhism. Returning to Japan, Suzuki eventually became a college professor. In 1921, he started the Eastern Buddhist Society, which published a scholarly journal on Buddhism written in English.

At 80 years old, Suzuki returned to the United States to teach at New York City's Columbia University. His lectures exposed many young Americans to Buddhism for the first time. Through his writings and his lectures, Suzuki influenced major Western thinkers, such as psychologist Carl Jung. He also touched many of the artists who helped form Beat Zen. In person, Suzuki impressed Americans with his simple and humble ways. Suzuki died in 1966, as the American Zen movement he helped create was still growing.

C. T. Shen (b. 1913)

A successful businessman in China and Hong Kong, Chia Theng Shen did not begin his true Buddhist studies until after he arrived in the United States in 1952. He continued his business endeavors while aiding the rebirth of Chinese Buddhism in his adopted country.

Shen studied electrical engineering in China and briefly served in the Chinese government before starting his own shipping company. In his personal life, Shen was drawn to the dharma's stress on ending suffering and promoting peace. In 1964, he helped found the Buddhist Association of the United States (BAUS), based at the Temple of Enlightenment in the Bronx, New York. BAUS now also has its own monastery in upstate New York.

Several years later, he launched the Institute for Advanced Studies of World Religions in New York. Shen has tried to bring together American Buddhists from all traditions. His donations of land and money have been used to start the Buddhist Text Translation Society in San Francisco, a Tibetan Buddhist monastery in New York, and the Bodhi House, on Long Island, where Buddhists from different schools hold retreats.

Shen has also written and spoken about Buddhism. He has extensively studied the Diamond Sutra, one of the most important sutras in Mahayana Buddhism. It focuses on nonduality and impermanence. For his entry in *Who's Who in America*, Shen wrote, "To benefit all human beings and to work toward freeing them from fear is my goal."

Havanpola Ratanasara (1920–2000)

The Venerable Havanpola Ratanasara was one of the leading Theravada Buddhists in the United States. He tried to bring together the different schools of Buddhism in America, as well as reach out to followers of other faiths.

Born in Sri Lanka, Ratanasara joined a monastery at age 12 and was ordained eight years later. He attended university in his homeland,

A force for unity
A native of Sri Lanka, Ven. Havanpola Ratanasara worked for more than two decades in the United States to help bring Buddhists of many traditions together.

the United States, and Great Britain, and he eventually earned a Ph.D. in education. He worked as a teacher and in 1957 was a representative for Sri Lanka at the United Nations.

In 1980, Ratanasara emigrated to the United States and settled in California. Almost immediately he began to encourage dialogue among Buddhists in America. He also looked at the issues ethnic Buddhists faced as they tried to practice their religion in a country without a strong Buddhist tradition.

In its obituary in 2000 for Ratanasara, the *Los Angeles Times* quoted him as posing the questions, "How can we become Americanized, yet hold to the core of Buddhism? How can we develop an American Buddhism, which will be vital and appropriate to this society and still retain our individual, unique traditions?"

With Karl Springer, a convert Buddhist, Ratanasara started the American Buddhist Congress in 1987. It was meant to answer Ratanasara's search for a way to build an American Buddhist tradition that honored the different schools of Buddhism and the different ethnic groups who practice Buddhism in the United States. The following year, Ratanasara ordained a Thai woman living in America, helping to revive the role of nuns in Theravada Buddhism. While working in this country, Ratanasara also kept ties to several monasteries in Sri Lanka and founded the International Institute of Buddhist Studies there.

Ruth Denison (b. 1922)

Ruth Denison was one of the first Americans to learn *vipassana* in Asia and begin teaching it in the United States. She also led the first Buddhist retreats for women only. Denison is seen as someone willing to use a wide variety of means to spread the dharma in the West.

Denison was born in eastern Germany and was working as a schoolteacher when World War II began. During the war, she endured bombings. When the war ended, she was sent to a Russian prison camp, where she was raped by soldiers. Denison relied on her faith (she was raised a Christian) to survive her ordeals.

During the 1950s, Denison came to the United States, where she met her future husband. He and Denison became interested in Zen and went to Asia to study. In Asia, Denison was attracted to *vipassana*. In Burma, she studied with U Ba Khin (1899–1971), who eventually gave her transmission so she could teach in the West. Denison, however, was reluctant to teach, and she continued to study meditation and Buddhism before she finally opened the Dhamma Dena Meditation Center in California (the center is named for an important female Buddhist teacher who lived 2,500 years ago). Denison later opened another retreat in Germany, and she has taught at the Insight Meditation Society in Massachusetts.

Denison's teacher wanted his students to be aware of their bodies when they meditate, and she has followed that emphasis. Her methods include using sounds and music and meditating while walking, running, jumping, and rolling on the ground. In a Spring 1997 interview with *Insight* magazine Denison said, "What I do is strictly within the prescribed bounds of Buddha's teachings—using the body and its sensations as a vehicle for mindfulness training...."

Gary Snyder (b. 1930)

An inspiration to Jack Kerouac in his book *The Dharma Bums*, Gary Snyder might not be as well known to most Americans as some of the other Beat writers of the 1950s. But among poets, Snyder is widely respected for his skills, and in his Zen practice he is a devoted Buddhist who has worked to spread the dharma in the West.

Snyder was already a poet and a Buddhist when he met Jack Kerouac and Allen Ginsberg in 1955. The next year, Snyder made the first of several trips to Japan to study Zen. He continued his studies throughout the 1960s and also published several books of poetry.

Snyder eventually built a home in California and concentrated on writing. His 1974 collection of poems, *Turtle Island*, won the Pulitzer Prize, and he has won several other writing awards. He has also been honored for his devotion to Buddhism. In 1998, a Japanese Buddhist organization gave him the Buddhism Transmission Award for his efforts to help Americans understand Buddhism. As an engaged Buddhist, Snyder supports environmental causes and the elimination of nuclear weapons.

Hakuyu Taizan Maezumi (1931–1995)

Hakuyu Taizan Maezumi helped bring together the Rinzai and Soto schools of Buddhism in the United States. Through him, a number of Americans received transmission of the dharma in Soto, and he founded a number of Zen temples in North America and Europe.

Born in 1931 in Japan, Maezumi was ordained a Soto monk at age 11. He studied at both universities and monasteries in Japan, and in 1955 he received dharma transmission from Hakujun Kuroda. Later he was given the title Inka, or teacher, from a master in the Rinzai tradition and from the founder of the Three Treasures Association.

In 1956, Maezumi came to Los Angeles to serve as a priest at the main Soto temple in the United States. Maezumi helped spread Soto Zen among converts, and in 1967 he opened the Zen Center of Los Angeles. He married an American woman and began raising a family in his adopted home.

Maezumi started six official Soto temples in the West, and a number of others are associated with that tradition. Some of the better-known convert priests who received transmission from him are John Daido Loori of New York's Zen Mountain Monastery, and Bernard Tetsugen Glassman, head of the Zen Community of New York. In all,

Vipassana Trio

The Insight Meditation Society (IMS) of Barre, Massachusetts, is one of the premier *vipassana* centers in the West. Its founders—Jack Kornfield (b.1945), Sharon Salzberg (b.1951), and Joseph Goldstein (b. 1944)—all studied with Asian masters before starting the center in 1975. Ruth Denison is one of the many well-known teachers to work at IMS.

Students can come for weekend classes or stay for months to deepen their practice. Salzberg and Goldstein are still at IMS, while Kornfield helped open a new retreat center, Spirit Rock, in California, where he is based. These three, along with Denison, deserve much of the credit for building *vipassana* practice in the United States.

Sharon Salzberg, Joseph Goldstein, and Jack Kornfield are shown at the 1979 Teaching Authorization Ceremony with Burmese master Venerable Mahasi Aayadaw and his monks.

Maezumi passed transmission to 12 Americans. These priests are associated in the White Plum Sangha, and they have already begun transmitting the dharma to a second generation of American Buddhists. Maezumi also ordained 68 priests and gave the lay precepts to more than 500 people.

Maezumi was also interested in the scholarly side of Zen Buddhism. In 1976, he started the Kuroda Institute for the Study of Buddhism and Human Values. The institute sponsors conferences and publishes books through the University of Hawaii Press.

Pema Chodron (b. 1936)

A former student of Chogyam Trungpa, Buddhist nun Pema Chodron is one of the most influential convert Buddhists in the United States. Head of the Gampo Abbey in Nova Scotia, Canada, she spreads Tibetan Buddhism through her writings and lectures.

Chodron was born Deirdre Blomfield-Brown in New York City. In her mid-30s, after a career as an elementary school teacher, she traveled to France and met her first guru. In 1972, she met Trungpa and began studying with him the next year. Ordained a novice nun in 1974, she became a full nun in 1981. Three years later, she took over as director of Gampo Abbey.

In her work, Chodron has often focused on *lojong* and the *paramitas*, practices designed to strengthen *bodhicitta*, or an "awakened heart"—compassion for others. Her books include *Start Where You Are* (1994) and *When Things Fall Apart* (2000). *Start Where You Are* is a detailed look at *lojong*, which includes *tonglen*, or taking in the pain of others through meditation and sending out compassion. In the book, Chodron writes that *lojong* must start with the individual practitioner: "…it is unconditional compassion for ourselves that leads naturally to unconditional compassion for others."

Chogyam Trungpa (1939–1987)

Chogyam Trungpa was one of the most popular—and controversial—Asian Buddhists to teach in the United States. He helped shape the strong interest in Tibetan Buddhism that remains today. He also introduced his own secular philosophical approach to life, Shambhala, that combines Buddhist ideas with other Tibetan and Indian traditions. A recent survey of religious leaders and scholars placed Trungpa

second on a list of the most important religious innovators of the 20th century.

While very young, Trungpa was identified as a *tulku* in the Kagyu lineage. (He also studied in the Nyingma and Rimed traditions.) He began his serious religious studies at age eight. In 1959, Trungpa joined other Tibetan lamas as they left their homeland to escape the Chinese invasion. He settled in India before going to Great Britain to study.

In 1967, he opened a Tibetan Buddhist study center in Scotland. Within two years, however, he gave up his vows as a monk and began to dress and act like a Westerner. He married and came to North America in 1970. Trungpa set up a Buddhist center in Vermont, then traveled extensively across the United States, speaking on Tibetan Buddhism. He also wrote several influential books that introduced many Americans to sitting meditation and the Buddha's teachings. Trungpa was hailed for his ability to explain Eastern ideas to a Western audience.

Trungpa eventually settled in Boulder, Colorado, where he opened the Naropa Institute. Trungpa stressed the idea of "cutting through spiritual materialism," which was the title of one of his most important books. Seeking enlightenment, he said, can create its own problems of attachment, of an "ego-centered version of spirituality." People might think they are approaching Buddhahood, but instead they are using their practice to boost their image of the self. Trungpa tried to help his students avoid this pitfall. In his personal life, Trungpa did not fit some students' image of the typical Asian Buddhist teacher. Trungpa smoked cigarettes, had sex with some of his students, and drank heavily. Trungpa wanted his students to see that a person could have true spirituality and secular, even "bad" habits, at the same time.

In 1986, Trungpa moved to Nova Scotia, Canada, where he had already founded a monastery, Gampo Abbey. He died the next year, and his organization, which came to be called Shambhala International, initially struggled under the control of his successor, Osel Tendzin. Today, however, Shambhala thrives, along with its practice and retreat centers in North America and Europe.

Tina Turner (b.1939)

During the mid 1970s, when Tina Turner's life began to crumble, she turned to Nichiren Buddhism as taught by Soka Gakkai, for comfort. Her new faith gave her the strength to end an abusive marriage and begin a new phase of her successful musical career.

Poet Practice

One of Chogyam Trungpa's most famous lay students was Allen Ginsberg (1926–1997). Although associated with the Beat Zen of the 1950s, Ginsberg's most serious Buddhist studies were in Tibetan Buddhism. Ginsberg began working with Trungpa in 1971, and often took retreats several weeks long to silently meditate. Ginsberg also taught at the Naropa Institute.

In March 1997, Ginsberg learned he was dying of cancer. He wrote what he called a funeral poem, which was read after his death. Its lines, as quoted in the summer 1997 issue of *Tricycle* magazine, include the passage reproduced on the right.

Many of Ginsberg's Buddhist friends, including his teacher Gelek Rinpoche and composer Philip Glass, were at his bed when he died. These guests performed several Tibetan rituals designed to help a Buddhist pass peacefully from this life into the next state of existence.

gone gone gone
won't be back today
gone gone gone
just like yesterday
gone gone gone
isn't anymore
gone to the other shore
gone gone gone
it wasn't here to stay

Keeping the Buddhist beat
*Popular singer Tina Turner
turned to Buddhism to help
her overcome a crisis in her
life. She remains an active
practitioner.*

Turner was born in a small town in Tennessee. As a teenager, she began performing with her future husband, Ike Turner, as a backup singer in his group, the Kings of Rhythm. By the early 1960s, the group was renamed the Ike and Tina Turner Revue and Tina was out front, singing lead and strutting across the stage. By the late 1960s, the band had several hit songs and had appeared often on national television programs.

Offstage, however, Turner endured severe beatings from her abusive husband. In 1974, Turner was introduced to Soka Gakkai and began chanting—sometimes as much as four hours a day. Slowly, she realized her career could survive without Ike, and that her physical survival depended on leaving him. They divorced in 1978.

As the 1980s started, Turner began appearing with different rock and roll stars, such as Rod Stewart and the Rolling Stones. Her solo career took off, and her album *Private Dancer* was one of the most successful records of the decade. She also acted in such movies as *Mad Max: Thunderdome*. Turner continues to record, perform, and follow her Buddhist practice.

Robert Thurman (b. 1941)

In some circles, Robert Thurman is best known as the father of actress Uma Thurman. But Thurman is also one of the most respected lay Buddhists in the United States, a scholar who actively brings his Buddhist beliefs into discussions on how to improve American society.

As a college student, Thurman left Harvard University to travel through India. Back in the United States, he met a Tibetan monk who stirred his interest in Vajrayana Buddhism. Thurman returned to India and met the Dalai Lama, who ordained him as a monk in 1964.

Scholar and teacher
Robert Thurman is among the most well-known Buddhist teachers in the United States. He was also the first American to be ordained a Tibetan Buddhist monk.

As the first American Tibetan-Buddhist monk, Thurman returned to the United States, where he gave up the monastic life so he could study and teach Buddhism. He eventually earned a Ph.D. from Harvard. In 1987, Thurman and actor Richard Gere founded Tibet House to draw attention to China's political domination of Tibet and to promote Tibetan culture.

Thurman has translated several Tibetan texts into English. He also wrote *Inner Revolution: Life, Liberty, and the Pursuit of Real Happiness*. This 1998 book reflects Thurman's belief that the enlightenment of individuals through Buddhism can lead to great political and social change—enlightenment on a vast scale.

Oliver Stone (b. 1946)

Unlike Martin Scorsese and Bernardo Bertolucci, two famous filmmakers who made movies about Tibetan Buddhism, director Oliver Stone has practiced Buddhism. Although known for films that feature violence, Stone's *Heaven and Earth* explored Vietnamese Buddhism, and Stone's work on the film led to his starting to meditate in the Mahayana tradition.

Stone was born in New York City, the son of wealthy parents. Unlike some privileged young men of his generation, Stone voluntarily joined the U.S. Army and served during the Vietnam War. He explored that war and its morality in his first widely acclaimed film, *Platoon* (1986), which won the Academy Award for Best Picture. Stone also won an award as Best Director. His other hit films include *Wall Street* (1987), *Born on the Fourth of July* (1989), *Natural Born Killers* (1994), *JFK* (1991), and *Any Given Sunday* (1999).

In *Heaven and Earth* (1993), Stone focused on the lives of a Vietnam veteran and his Buddhist Vietnamese wife. Stone called the movie a Buddhist film, because it shows the importance of the religion to the wife. She shows a sense of compassion and forgiveness despite the difficulties she experiences. During production, Stone explored Buddhism, meeting with Tibetan lamas in Nepal and monks in Thailand. In *Tricycle*'s Spring 1994 issue he said that he hoped more Americans would discover Buddhism. "Buddhism can only be good for the country," he said, "—for the political, social, and cultural ethic. It has a beneficent, self-realization energy that can only help America heal."

The Future of
Buddhism in America

SEVERAL SCHOLARS HAVE COMPARED BUDDHISM IN AMERICA TO A teenager. Although is is an ancient faith elsewhere, in the United States Buddhism is no longer a child, but it is not quite fully mature. It is still changing as it tries to shape its identity. Change has been an important part of Buddhism since its founding more than 2,500 years ago. As Buddhism spread beyond India, it picked up ideas from different cultures and religious traditions. In the United States, Buddhism has changed again, while it has also influenced the dominant culture of the nation—one traditionally shaped by both Judeo-Christian and secular values.

As this book has tried to show, Buddhism comes in many forms, and all are represented in the United States. This variety of practices makes it harder to define Buddhism in the United States than it would be in some Asian countries, where just one form or vehicle dominates.

American Buddhism is also shaped by the different ethnic and racial groups that practice it. The United States has been called a melting pot—a place where immigrants eventually lose their cultural differences and form a new American culture. The country has also been compared to a salad bowl—the different ethnic groups live side by side in one "dish," but they do not really blend together.

PRECEDING PAGE
Happy birthday, Buddha
Monks, teachers, and Buddhists from all different forms of Buddhism came together in 2000 in Los Angeles to celebrate the Buddha's birthday. America is perhaps the first country in history in which all the forms of Buddhism are practiced.

American Buddhism has shown a little of both of these tendencies. The different schools and traditions are separate, and even followers of the same tradition might be set apart, ethnic from convert. Yet one of the trends in American Buddhism is a movement to bring the different traditions together, to find the essence of the Buddha's message that remains constant. And this movement has developed next to a growing attempt to bridge the cultural gap between ethnic and convert Buddhists. These efforts will continue in the years to come, although some Buddhist scholars wonder how complete they will be.

Ethnic Buddhism

All the major religions practiced in the United States could be called "immigrant" religions. Native American beliefs and practices were the only ones that developed in the United States. American Buddhism was greatly shaped by immigrants from one part of the world, people who for many years were left out of the country's political life and economic success. The association of Buddhism with a minority group that faced legal discrimination held back the acceptance of Buddhism in mainstream American culture.

By the 21st century, however, Asian immigrants and their descendants had made great strides in achieving a fuller place in American society. Their rise helped establish Buddhism as a major religion. So did the presence of respected Asian Buddhist scholars and religious leaders, such as D. T. Suzuki, Thich Nhat Hanh, and the Dalai Lama. The huge increase in the number of immigrants coming to the United States from traditionally Buddhist countries also played a part. Immigration from Asia began to drop off at the end of the 20th century, but Asians and Asian Americans still represented a fast-growing part of the U.S. population. The Buddhists in that population will continue to play an active role in American life.

There is a chance, of course, that Buddhist immigrants who prosper in the United States might not keep their native faith. During America's history, children and grandchildren of immigrants have often converted to other religions, especially as they marry people of other faiths. That trend might continue with Asian-American Buddhists as well. Or perhaps some ethnic Buddhists will embrace the more Westernized Buddhism emerging in the convert communities rather than following traditional practices from their homelands.

The Convert Community

The growing interest in Buddhism noted in the U.S. media usually focuses on converts to the faith. Throughout its history in America, Buddhism has appealed to a small group of influential people: scholars, artists, and intellectuals. These people help define the direction a culture takes, at least at one level.

At the other level is pop culture: music, television, and films. Although Buddhism is touched on in these media, sometimes the treatment lacks depth. Companies use Buddhist words and images in their ads, and the media report on which star practices Buddhism, but the deeper meaning of the dharma is ignored. Committed convert Buddhists still have to educate the larger culture about their faith and the role it can play in America. That process has already begun and will continue in the decades ahead.

Some leading Buddhists, however, say their goal in America should not be to go out and win more converts to the faith. In a Spring 2000 interview with *Tricycle*, Robert Thurman quoted the Dalai Lama's feelings on this issue: "I don't want you to be a Buddhist, necessarily. It's better if you learn from Buddhism and keep connected to the religions of your family, of your community, and develop the

DEDICATED MONK

Thanissaro Bhikkhu (above) was born Geoffrey DeGraff. After graduating from college in 1971, he taught in Thailand, where he studied Theravada Buddhism. Ordained a monk in 1976, he later helped start the Metta Forest Monastery. Thanissaro believes the traditional ways of learning the dharma are important for Americans. He told *Insight Magazine Online* in Spring, 2000, "There is no real substitute for spending time in close contact with a really wise person, but the suttas [sutras] can often be the next best thing—especially in a country like ours where wise people, in the Buddhist sense of the term, are so few and far between."

positive qualities that Buddhism would like you to develop within those settings."

Part of that process is reflected through engaged Buddhism. The goals of engaged Buddhists—promoting peace, protecting the environment, achieving social justice—appeal to many Americans who do not necessarily want to meditate or chant sutras. The political and social activity of Buddhists gives them meaningful contact with the larger American culture and brings Buddhist ideals into debates on public policy.

The Major Issues for the Future

Buddhist scholars usually agree that American and Buddhist values are blending to create a new form of Buddhism—a trend that will continue. The United States has more concern for equality between the sexes than most Asian countries traditionally have. That push for equality is seen in the growing number of American women ordained as priests and nuns and given leadership roles in various Buddhist organizations. American Buddhists have also tried to bring more democracy to a religion that has traditionally been very authoritarian. American Buddhists still have to balance this desire with the crucial role masters and lamas play in handing down the wisdom of Buddhism.

Not all converts agree on how to address these issues and develop an American Buddhism. Lama Surya Das (b.1950), a convert to Tibetan Buddhism, has called for a broad approach that draws on such things as equality, democracy, and social engagement. In his writing, Surya Das has called for a "simplified" Buddhism for Americans. Some critics see this kind of Buddhism as blending too much with New Age ideas, or designed to make Buddhism easier for converts to accept.

Convert Buddhists such as Thanissaro Bhikkhu (b.1949), however, see the value in the monastic tradition and staying close to the original forms of Buddhism. Thanissaro Bhikkhu was named the abbot of the Metta Forest Monastery, in southern California, in 1993. He has translated many texts from Pali into English and posted them on the Internet.

Thanissaro is one of many American converts in both the Theravada and Mahayana vehicles who do not want a "new" American Buddhism. In this Americanized Buddhism, he told *Insight Magazine Online*, "things get passed on . . . from one generation of teachers to the next, until the message gets garbled beyond recognition." Thanissaro

Bhikkhu says too many Americans are not willing to make the sacrifices true Buddhism demands.

Some American Buddhists see a third way emerging between the "new" Buddhism and the old. They believe practitioners can find a middle way between the monastic lifestyle and lay practice. Some meditation centers and retreats work closely with members who spend most of their time in the lay world, yet still take time throughout the year to live as monks. Most experts seem to agree, however, that convert Buddhism will remain mostly a lay movement. And, as has happened during the last few decades, more Americans will meditate and embrace Buddhist notions without taking the precepts or calling themselves Buddhists—just as the Dalai Lama suggested.

Reaching Out to Other Faiths

The 1893 World's Parliament of Religions attempted to bring together great teachers from all faiths. The effort was meant to broaden Americans' spiritual knowledge. One hundred years later, a second parliament was held in Chicago, attracting about 8,000 people and reflecting a continuing desire to build bridges between the followers of different faiths.

American Buddhists play a large role in the interfaith movement, and likely will continue to do so. Thubten Chodron (b.1950), a convert Tibetan Buddhist nun from Los Angeles, has written on this movement and taken part in interfaith activities. In 2002, she attended the Second Gethsemani Encounter, held at Gethsemani Abbey in Kentucky. Buddhists from several traditions, both convert and ethnic, met with Catholic monks to discuss the similarities of their respective religions. The meeting was part of a dialogue between Catholic monastics and Buddhists that began many years before, led by the Trappist monk Thomas Merton.

Thich Nhat Hanh has also sought to link Christianity and Buddhism. In his popular 1996 book *Living Buddha, Living Christ*, Hanh writes that people should experience even the most sacred acts of other faiths. He saw nothing wrong with a Buddhist receiving the Eucharist— the body of Christ—during a Catholic mass. The sharing of beliefs and rituals, Hanh believes, can help build peace.

As noted in chapter 3, a large number of American Buddhists converted from Judaism, and they have tried to forge links between

ZEN CHRISTIAN MONK

Thomas Merton (1915–1968) was a monk, mystic, and scholar with a wide interest in Asian religions and philosophies. He was one of the first American Catholics to appreciate and write about Zen, although he never abandoned his faith in Christianity. Merton lived at Gethsemani Abbey in Kentucky. In 1968, Merton left his monastery for the first time in decades and traveled to Asia, where he met the Dalai Lama and other Tibetan lamas. He died on the trip, before reaching his goal of meeting Zen *roshis* in Japan.

their new faith and Judaism. Thubten Chodron was raised Jewish, and she has met with rabbis, who are divided in their opinions about Jews who convert. Some rabbis are fearful of the trend, while others see that Buddhist meditation practices can be helpful. Her own beliefs probably reflect the thinking of many converts: "I see good points and bad points in both Western and Asian cultures and values," she wrote on her web site (www.thubtenchodron.org), "and am somehow trying to incorporate the best of both into my personal life."

The continuing exchanges between Buddhism and other faiths will probably lead more Americans to strive for the same goal, and to play a part in making American Buddhism distinct from its Asian roots.

The Next Convert Generation

The baby boom generation—people born between 1946 and 1964—fueled the growth of American convert Buddhism. By the beginning of the 21st century, the members of this generation were graying, and some scholars wondered what direction convert Buddhism would take.

Richard Hughes Seager, in his book *Buddhism in America*, recounted a conversation with a prominent American Buddhist who noted Buddhist parents often did not want to "lay their Buddhism on their children." This, Seager points out, is very different from the immigrant experience, where children go to the temple and participate in all parts of their family's religious life, at least through their teen years.

Young Americans who are not Asian, however, are turning to Buddhism on their own. For its Spring 1997 issue, *Tricycle* interviewed several young members of the Rochester Zen Center. They all had become Buddhists in their late teens or early 20s. They shared some traits: All had parents who either divorced or were unmarried. And according to interviewee Lhasa Ray, they all shared "a common sense of powerlessness or despair that has been with us since the very beginning." For these and other young people, the dharma offers a way to confront the despair and suffering they see around them.

In 2001, Sumi Loundon published *Blue Jean Buddha*, a series of essays by young American Buddhists. Some were raised Buddhists, others converted. The essays looked at common concerns of young people, such as relationships and finding jobs, through a Buddhist perspective. Most of these young Buddhists practiced engaged Buddhism and tried to adapt the dharma to American life, as the baby boomers

TARGETING YOUTH

Of the main Buddhist groups in the United States, Soka Gakkai makes the most effort to reach out specifically to young Americans. The SGI-USA web site (www.sgi-usa.org) features splashy graphics and upbeat music on its page for youth activities. Soka Gakkai has a program for youths called Victory Over Violence, which tries to reduce violence among teens and promote racial and ethnic harmony.

did before them. Loundon writes, "While taking a step on the Buddhist path may feel radical in many ways, it is no longer necessarily seen that way by the culture at large." She also notes that during the 1960s, few people had heard of the Dalai Lama. By the 1990s, his public appearances in New York drew tens of thousands of people.

Future generations of ethnic and convert Buddhists will have many choices. They can follow the more traditional approaches practiced in Asia and in many monasteries in the United States. They can work to develop the Americanized Buddhism that has emerged since World War II. They can choose from within different schools of Buddhism, mix the traditions to suit their liking, or blend the dharma with other faiths. Buddhism in America, like the country itself, presents diversity and choice.

As a faith, it might be even harder to define what exactly American Buddhism is. But what will remain constant for all Buddhists is the acceptance of the Buddha's Four Noble Truths and the hope he offered to end human suffering.

Under the big tent
Demonstrating the increasingly visible role of Buddhism in America, these Vietnamese Buddhist nuns took part in a ceremony honoring victims of the September 11, 2001, terrorist attacks on the United States.

GLOSSARY

anatman non-self, the essence of each person that can reach nirvana

arhat in Theravada Buddhism, a person who is sure to reach nirvana

bhikkhu a fully ordained Buddhist monk

bhikkhuni a fully ordained Buddhist nun

bodhicitta "awakened heart," or compassion for others

bodhisattva in Mahayana Buddhism, a person who delays attaining nirvana to help end the suffering of others

Ch'an the Chinese form of Zen Buddhism, which places great emphasis on meditation and mindfulness, or always being aware of what one is doing

cybersangha community of Buddhists who communicate through the Internet

dharma The teachings of Buddha, or Buddhism itself

dukkha suffering or dissatisfaction; the First Noble Truth

Eightfold Path Buddha's list of right actions and attitudes for his followers

Five Precepts vows taken by lay Buddhists when joining the faith

Four Noble Truths the core of Buddhism, as taught by Buddha: all existence is suffering; suffering is caused by desire and ignorance; suffering can end by letting go of craving; the way to do this is to follow the Eightfold Path

Gelugpa one of the four orders of monks in Tibetan Buddhism

guru Indian word for teacher

Hinayana the "lesser vehicle"; a dismissive name for Theravada

Jodo Shinshu form of Mahayana Buddhism developed by the Japanese monk Shinran

JuBu a Jewish person who embraces Buddhism, sometimes blending the two faiths

Kagyupa one of the four orders of monks in Tibetan Buddhism

karma actions and their results

koan in Zen, a puzzle or story students contemplate to help them attain enlightenment

lama a teacher in Tibetan Buddhism

Mahayana the "great vehicle"; one of the three major forms of Buddhism

mandala a sacred image of the forces of nature

mantra a word or sound chanted during meditation

merit gaining good karma by performing acts of compassion and charity

mutra specific body positions that help achieve enlightenment

Nichiren a Japanese monk who left his order to form a new branch of Buddhism, now named for him

nirvana liberation from attachments and the cycle of reincarnation; the ultimate goal of Buddhists

Nyingma one of the four orders of monks in Tibetan Buddhism

Pure Land a form of Mahayana Buddhism that stresses reaching a heaven-like place called the Pure Land

Rimé a recent tradition in Tibetan Buddhism that tries to bring together ideas from the four major orders of monks

rinpoche a term of respect usually reserved for a teacher

Rinzai one of the two major schools of Zen Buddhism

roshi a Japanese word meaning "venerable master"; a title accorded a Zen master

Sakyamuni "sage of the Sakya clan"; one of the names for Buddha

Sakyapa one of the four orders of monks in Tibetan Buddhism

samsara the wheel of life and death, or the cycle of dying and being reborn

sangha the community of Buddhist believers

Soka Gakkai a lay organization once associated with Nichiren Buddhist priests, now on its own

S'on the Korean form of Ch'an or Zen Buddhism

Soto one of the two major schools of Zen Buddhism

stupa a Buddhist shrine where relics are kept

sunim Korean word for teacher

sunyata emptiness; a key concept in Mahayana Buddhism

sutra scripture or teaching from Buddha

tantra sacred text or teaching ("tantric" is the adjective)

Tathagatha "thus gone"; one of the names for Buddha

Theravada the oldest form of Buddhism, based on the first Buddhist writings in the Pali language

thich Vietnamese term of respect for a teacher

tonglen Tibetan meditation in which the practitioner breathes in the suffering of others and sends out love

Triple Jewel Buddha, dharma, *sangha*; the essence of Buddhist practice

tulku a reincarnated Tibetan lama

Vajrayana the Diamond Vehicle; one of the three major forms of Buddhism

vipassana a form of meditation practiced in Theravada Buddhism; also called insight meditation

zazen form of meditation used in Zen Buddhism

Zen a form of Mahayana Buddhism developed in China and first practiced in Japan that stresses meditation

zendo the hall where Zen Buddhists meditate

TIME LINE

1844	Chinese Buddhists in San Francisco open the first Buddhist temple in the United States. *The Dial*, a New England literary magazine, publishes the first American translation of a Buddhist sutra.
1880	Henry Steel Olcott and Helena Petrorna Blavatsky become the first European Americans to publicly declare their faith in Buddhism.
1893	The World's Parliament of Religions, held in Chicago, introduces many Americans to the various Buddhist traditions.
1899	The first Jodo Shinshu priests arrive in San Francisco. D. T. Suzuki translates some of the teachings of his Zen master, Soyen Shaku, for an American audience.
1924	Immigration Act denies entry into America to virtually all Asians.
1932	Dwight Goddard publishes *A Buddhist Bible*, which includes writings from all three vehicles.
1945	Jodo Shinshu Buddhists rename their organization the Buddhist Churches of America.
1950	D. T. Suzuki returns to the United States to teach at Columbia University, fueling the growth of Beat Zen.
1955	Geshe Wangyal is the first Tibetan Buddhist monk to settle in the United States.
1960	Daisaku Ikeda, president of Soka Gakkai, comes to the United States to promote Nichiren Buddhism.
1960s	Vietnamese Buddhist monk Thich Nhat Hanh introduces the idea of socially engaged Buddhism to the West.
1965	Congress passes a new law that allows increased immigration from Asia.
1966	The first Theravada temple in the United States opens in Washington, D.C.
1975	The end of the Vietnam War leads to a large flow of Buddhist refugees coming from Southeast Asia to the United States.
1978	The Buddhist Peace Fellowship is formed.
1987	Havanpola Ratanasara cofounds the American Buddhist Congress to promote connections among the Buddhists traditions in the United States.
1997	The Hollywood movie *Kundun* explores the early life of the 14th Dalai Lama.

RESOURCES

Reading List

Dhammapada: The Sayings of Buddha, Translated by Thomas Cleary. New York: Bantam Books, 1995.

Fields, Rick, *How the Swans Came to the Lake: A Narrative History of Buddhism in America*, 3rd ed. Boston: Shambhala, 1992.

Gyatso, Tenzin, the 14th Dalai Lama, *Freedom in Exile: The Autobiography of the Dalai Lama*. New York: HarperCollins, 1990.

Kherdian, David, ed., *Beat Voices: An Anthology of Beat Poetry*. New York: Henry Holt, 1995.

Loundon, Sumi, *Blue Jean Buddha: Voices of Young Buddhists*. Somerville, Mass.: Wisdom Publications, 2001.

Man-tu Lee, Anthony, and David Weiss, *Zen in 10 Simple Lessons*. New York: Barron's, 2002.

Wangu, Madhu Bazaz, *Buddhism,* rev. ed. New York: Facts On File, 2002

Weisman, Arinna, and Jean Smith, *The Beginner's Guide to Insight Meditation*. New York: Bell Tower, 2001.

Resources on the Web

Access to Insight
www.accesstoinsight.org/index.html
An online source for Theravada texts, maintained by a lay practitioner.

Buddhanet.net
www.buddhanet.net/budnetp.htm
This comprehensive site offers links to Buddhist centers around the world and some basic teachings of the Buddha.

Buddhist Peace Fellowship
www.bpf.org
This site offers the latest news on the activities of the Buddhist Peace Fellowship, as well as selected contents from *Turning Wheel* magazine.

The Tibet Center
www.thetibetcenter.org/index.html
The center, founded in 1975 in New York, promotes Tibetan Buddhism and supports Tibetan political independence from China.

Tricycle.com: The Buddhist Review Online
www.tricycle.com
Online home of the prominent Buddhist magazine *Tricycle*, with articles from the current and past issues.

Zen Buddhism WWW Virtual Library
www.ciolek.com/WWWVL-Zen.html
An in-depth source of information on all forms of Buddhism, this site has Zen writings, koan study guides, and links to Zen centers.

INDEX

Note: *Italic* page numbers refer to illustrations.